Second Wind

Second Wind

Meditations and Prayers for Today's Women

Margaret Anne Huffman

BAKER BOOK HOUSE
Grand Rapids, Michigan 49516

Copyright 1990 by
Baker Book House Company

ISBN: 0-8010-4347-6

Illustrations by Jack Brouwer

Printed in the United States of America

For **Gary**

". . . this is my beloved
and my friend."

Song of Solomon 5:16b

and
Lynn, Rob, and **Beth,**

the enrichment

Contents

Introduction

The Hermit Crab

He was such a small, scrawny hermit crab that he was a seventy-five-cent bargain. The children and I carried him home from the pet store in a plastic bag filled with sea water. Gently, we emptied him into a new ocean, our thirty-gallon salt water aquarium, as close to our favorite seashore as we could come in the landlocked Midwest.

Scarcely pausing to notice his new surroundings, he skittered over the sand, antennae charting succulent algae to eat later. Using his fierce claws, he tugged himself up the bubbling air hose as it spread its miniature waves across the water's surface. Feasting on a chunk of the lush, hairy green food, he shared it with a tiny starfish nearby.

Watching his comic dances and insatiable appetite filled happy, welcome interludes in our busy lives as we visited his world atop the bookcase, which we passed daily on the way to the school bus, to work, to play.

One morning, however, when I clicked on the tank light to signal day for the artificial world, I discovered a shrunken, lifeless crab huddled against the coral.

How dull and ordinary the sea world seemed.

I fought an urge to turn off the light to slow the crimson, yellow, and blue fishes' games of tag. If only the darting, busy creatures would become still, it might lessen the absence of the clown, our crab.

Forlorn, we scooped him out with the dip net and tossed him out the door for the cat.

As I replaced the aquarium cover, however, I noticed a slight tremor from one of the empty shells strewn about the tank. Wildly vibrating antennae protruded from a large shell in friendly greeting. It was the crab, dressed in a new house preposterously too large for him.

The hastily summoned children and I laughed aloud at him.

He looked like a twelve-year-old in new Easter clothes with his lanky wrists peeking from a drooping jacket, and a safety pin to lap the back of the trousers puckering the seat.

Lugging his new shell proudly around the tank, he was frequently forced to rest. And, if we stood very still and silent, he would slip out of it and back into his old discarded smaller shell as if he'd forgotten something.

The children, intrigued, flipped to the *C*'s in the encyclopedia and checked out sea-creature books from the library. We discovered that our crab had molted his skin, which was what I'd found in the tank.

Hermit crabs live in discarded sea-snail shells, twisting their soft bodies into the spiral, with only their claws left outside to use as a tightly fitting front door. Leaving his constricting, too-small shell, our crab had leased a larger one to accommodate his new growth.

During the transition between shells, while his fresh, pink skin was not yet hardened, he was vulnerable. In a natural environment he would be defenseless, a delicacy for his enemies. But a crab that remains safe in an old shell, afraid to expose tender skin while searching for shells to trade, denies the need for growth. Gradually, it will choke itself to death, suffocated by security.

As soon as we realized that the crab was alive, I quickly retrieved what was actually just his skin. Later,

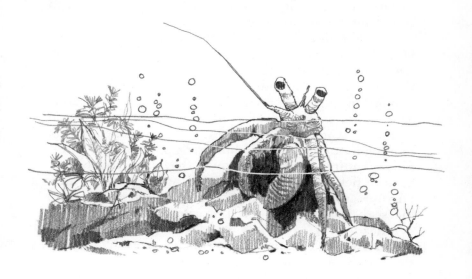

I embedded it in plastic to make a small paperweight. Anchoring bills and notes on my desk, it reminds me just how important are the in-between times.

Change, vulnerability: old shells, new ones that don't quite fit, and tender new skin are like our shriveled feelings of lifelessness and breathless gaspings in suffocation from our own squeezed, too-full days—times in each of our lives.

The tales I tell here are from my log of wanderings. They chart discoveries I've made as I groped for familiar landmarks. Like buoys strung against being buffeted by relentless gusts and tides, they mark my search for balance in life's ebb and flow.

The crab is an ingenious scavenger, a survivor, and an adventurer busily turning over shells, measuring them for future use. He struggles to tip over the conch shells and coral four times his size that are blocking his path. Inquisitive and hungry, he will retrieve a shred of shrimp carelessly dropped by fish who are contented to be fed and merely swim in circles.

And still, like the crab, I continue to tug and shove life's dailiness that often seems at least four times my size, assured that no thought is too tough or trivial for God's attention and redeeming companionship.

Not long ago, burrowed against a warm sand dune on the Outer Banks of North Carolina, like a crab myself, I watched the Atlantic Ocean come and go, sending in its frothy wake hundreds of skittering crabs. Silly creatures. Don't they know that the ocean will be back to tickle in ever-closer circles at the doors of their burrows until at last it floods them and sends them to the sea's floor? I wondered, dozing, as gulls gossiped overhead.

Just when it seems futile, ridiculous even, to push steadfastly on, when spirits falter like a crab weary from wrestling shells buried in wet sand at the shoreline, comes the gentle nudge from a sudden updraft of a drying, sifting air current, to hold us a little longer so that we can gain our second wind and keep going following an especially good laugh, a painfully hard cry.

I here encourage you to trust in the promise of the ever-present blowing of the Spirit across our lives—as constant as the breeze kicking up ruffles on the waves and stirring up the sands beneath the sea's surface to expose new shells, food for the journey, new possibilities that may well be hints from God. Breathe deeply, for there is enough of God's grace to take us the next step.

1

Tea Parties and Spaceships

Nibbling around the edges of a fancy mud pie, I wiped my lips with a pretend napkin. I lifted a cup of raindrop tea, not spilling a drop.

Teatime at the home of the queen.

Gowned in wrinkled red satin, a flowered hat perched atop her curls, her majesty offered me seconds. I accepted another gooey serving as gratefully as I had her invitation.

Ironing waited in the utility room, dishes in the sink, and my nap indefinitely. The scribbled invitation, engraved with five-year-old love, had lifted me from my routine into the extraordinary life of my child.

We chatted eye-to-eye as I sat scrunched in a child-sized chair in her tree house. Our laughter drifted across breezes teasing the maple-leaf roof.

Wiping her nose on a sleeve, she cried for her dead gray kitten, a subject previously avoided. Wide-eyed, she shared her fears about riding the big yellow school bus to kindergarten in the fall with the "really scary big kids."

Lifting the lid of her wooden treasure box, she let me touch, oh so carefully, the butterfly wings and cocoon kept nestled in a scrap of her infant quilt. We admired the faded reflection in a tarnished locket, a great-grandmother long gone. "But where?" she wondered. "With my kitten?"

We communed on her level, in her home, her space. Importantly private, it was as fragile as the butterfly wings she tenderly tucked away.

On other visits through the years, the children and I wriggled through blanket houses stretched across dining room chairs. Picnics were devoured on safari in the yard, expeditions braved through the wilds of the orchard. Not always earthbound, we sped beyond the stars in sofa cushion spaceships. Refrigerator carton rockets, catapulting us through the galaxies, gained on elusive space pirates.

Chattering squirrels and indignant sparrows are the only residents in the cobwebbed tree house now. The locket fell through a crack in the porch floor; the kitten's grave disappeared in the weeds.

But today I again visited her majesty, my third child, again at her invitation, grown more valuable because it extends from her teenage years. We journeyed on vibrations from a new rock album, to which Beth had casually suggested, "Come listen sometime." Once again, laundry, the house, my nap were put on hold—where they'd keep.

They would, but children don't.

In a blink, they've turned the corner. I stand in the dust, watching, wishing I'd done, said more.

Intrigued by today's music, though, we rested on her quilt-covered bed beneath smiles of poster lovers. Balanced precariously on closet shelves across the room were boxes of toys and dolls labeled and packed carefully away, innocence and fantasy stashed there, too.

Over the music, we chatted, discussing lyrics, rhythm, records versus tapes. And suddenly, we were considering her suspicion she's too fat, too tall, her braces too

shiny, hair too thin. And I learned, to my amazement,
she's planning to be a marine biologist.

Again, we met on her level, the only place to com-
mune with a child.

Years ago, while shopping, I dropped my purse.
Change rolled drunkenly across the floor. Bending to
retrieve my belongings, I looked up into the face of a
small child walking past. Together we crouched, surrounded by clamoring, bustling adults swarming above.

How, I marveled from my knees, can communication
happen?

It can when we stop, stoop down, and meet our children where they are: rock music, flash dancing, at tea
with the queen, or soaring through the skies with astro-
knights in shining armor.

In time, the armor tarnishes. Spaceships are
grounded on plains of reality, the mud pies return to
dust. And the dreamers vanish—exploring, struggling
with real pirates, flesh-and-blood battles of the spirit.

Then, on a Thursday midnight, a familiar message interrupts.

"Mom?" the quavering voice rises in descant above the college switchboard operator's crisp question, "Will you accept a collect call?"

"Of course," I stammer, still sleep drugged, heart pounding, throat scratchy with fearful possibilities.

"Mom, I'm so homesick . . . tests all day . . . no date for homecoming . . . my roommate snores. . . ."

Once again, across tea parties pressed between pages of memory, the invitation arrive.

We'll talk more, catching up, Friday when everyone comes home, a brief gathering of the scattered. Tacos have been requested for supper, lemon cake for dessert, favorites for the grownup table where we meet eye-to-eye, even though I'm now the one who has to look up to a broad-shouldered son, willowy daughters.

Now they bend to meet my gaze, still only an invitation away.

Prayer

Give me energy and patience, Lord, for those days when I simply cannot handle one more interruption and then here comes a child needing a hug, a scrape kissed, or a teenager comes with a record to play, a movie to debate, a joke to tell.

Help me see, Lord, that interruptions are sometimes disguised invitations—invitations into the lives of those we love.

Even in my tiredness keep me approachable, accessible, ready to venture into the world of another. For those invitations are not easily given; the guest list is brief and carefully screened.

And help me continue to do it while the children are young, the relationships full of wonder. And then when daydreams and pretend become reality, sometimes harsh and painful, I will still be invited in to share, to listen, to just be there as you are. Help me cherish the invitations, the glimpses into the often uncharted channels traveled by my children.

Help me, too, to honor their uniqueness, their separateness from me when the umbilical cords are broken by spaceships' thrust. Still, let us remain connected as I practice being a guest at their tables, a passenger in the capsules of their fantasies fueled by rockets of imagination, soaring into their days.

Give me energy, vision, and imagination, Lord.

Tomorrow: Canceled

The telephone rang just before noon. "Please hurry! They need us."

Members of a prayer group, we were being summoned beyond words into deeds. Two of our number had just lost a son down the dark pit of his despair.

I rearranged car pooling and turned off the eggs boiling for lunch's salad. No appetite now. Succumbing, though, to a gnawing hunger to see, to touch my own children, I detoured past their grade school on my way out of town. Safe; they appeared to be safe.

No words came as I cradled our friend in my arms like the lost child we had all become. Grief swept through the crowded but suddenly empty farmhouse.

Most of us simply stood around. Others sat or paced outside beneath the towering pines, mute in our guilt, our blindness to impending tragedy.

Throughout the day, like wind-up toys the bereaved parents recited their story as each newcomer hesitantly took their hands.

Dawn, they insisted, had looked like any other.

Up early, their tall young son showered and dressed for school and greeted the family when he came downstairs for breakfast. The collie, Laddie, took his place beside his master, resting a shaggy head on a blue-jeaned knee. The usual scraps were dropped for him under the table. Appreciatively, he licked the hand that stroked behind his ears.

A pleasant, smiling teenager, his fair hair had been bleached even whiter by the summer sun. This was to be a full year for him, his junior year. Sports, a girl friend, work on the farm after school—a promising year.

Breakfast was over with time to spare before the arrival of the school bus, they recalled. He returned to his bedroom to sit for a moment on the edge of his quilt-covered twin bed. Aiming carefully at his head, he pulled the trigger of his rifle, a recent birthday present. Death was instantaneous.

Alerted by the insistent honking of the waiting bus, his mother climbed the stairs and found him. The few lines neatly penciled on the back of a test paper his father showed us in bewilderment yielded no explanation, just a decision to "leave this rotten world."

The bus driver notified authorities and then delivered the rest of his students to school. The window seat third from the back was conspicuously empty, the students strangely silent.

The house made so quickly empty by death was filled during the remainder of the crisp fall afternoon as we washed dishes and stored the food that had begun arriving. Laddie refused to leave us and whimpered from his rug beside the door.

Some of our group cleaned the upstairs bedroom; the mattress and coverings were hauled to the dump by the deacons.

Our church was filled for a quiet memorial service. Fresh-faced classmates were jolted abruptly from their youthful stance of immortality. Their new vulnerability was worn tentatively and with care like a suit too large.

I watched from across the leaf-strewn slope as

arthritic grandparents gathered at the muddy edge of a cemetery plot they'd thought to occupy first. The truck couldn't wait until the shattered parents and bewildered friends left the cemetery before dumping its load of fresh dirt onto the bronze casket, onto their son, our friend.

Why?

The question reverberated from the high school corridors to family dinner tables to strangers in the community.

Why?

This was to have been a good year, the best so far. Yet, now, many of the times that had looked like successes or triumphs could be seen as threatening when we looked closer. They were tormented episodes, containing more pressure than the young man could endure.

He had hidden behind a brittle mask of quiet, secret desperation, keeping to himself the doubts, the half-formed fears and worries. Afraid to show any "weakness," he never knew the greatest strength is found in reaching out. The greater weakness is in secrets that are born and flourish in the gloom of isolation.

Now, with the clarity of vision that comes with hindsight, we who knew him could see tiny fragments of warning—oddly shaped and in themselves meaningless, but each piece a clue to disaster.

As it always does, time did pass. Like a tilted kaleidoscope, life once more shifted and rearranged itself. The mother updated her credentials and returned to work as a counselor. She vented her grief and fury on bureaucratic red tape in the local welfare office.

The father had to have two-thirds of his stomach removed, finding relief from his ulcer-eroded guilt in the unpalatable diet he was forced to follow. He, too, returned to work, but changed jobs. The solitary farm days were too full of glimpses of a small son following his father from tractor to field, barn to fence, each small step imitating the older man in his stride, in the unconscious tilt of a small blond head.

They avoided church for a while and never returned to our small group. All we could do, after a time, was name them in prayer.

Their marriage began a slow death, unspoken blame and criticisms depleting its strength. Separate rooms were monuments to failure.

It was uncertain whether or not this trend could be reversed. They were too willing to accept this new loss as payment for errors remembered and magnified. They visited the neatly kept grave at different times, unable to share their tears.

Why? was never answered to anyone's satisfaction and, of course, was rarely discussed openly. Clues remained obscured by the social taboos surrounding suicide. And politely sympathetic folk were just glad it had not happened to them even as they wondered if it could.

Prayer

O Lord, I never suspected. I never stopped talking, organizing, planning, teaching long enough to hear what he was trying to say. His music, poetry, aloofness were not maturity at all but rather the silently shrill cry of a tormented soul.

I can still see him, Lord, in his favorite corner of the fellowship room—a handsome teenager, a credit to the youth group, a prize pupil under my leadership.

But now he's gone, Lord, and I can only hope he is with you. Please ease his pain, the burden he carried of being so young, so frightened, so alone even in the midst of us all.

Ease my pain, too, and his parents'. And lead me to

know what to say to his friends, the other members of the youth group waiting, listening over Ping-Pong or pizza. Forgive our failure.

Help us all to learn how to listen, to hear what another is not able to say before it's too late.

3

Hobgoblins and Reindeer

I went shopping last week for Halloween candy and brought home three strands of blinking Christmas tree lights, a package of tinsel, holly-sprigged paper, and two dozen candy canes.

Trick-or-treaters may find slim pickings at my house, but Christmas carolers will be in luck.

Holidays were different when I was a child, before the time of blended seasons. Santa was not on hand to dance with Dracula. Easter eggs rolled *after* Valentine's Day then, and bathing suits appeared amidst tulips, not icicles. Pumpkins didn't nestle with sugarplums in those simpler years, and all seasons felt longer.

In my yesteryear, classmates and I savored seasonal changes in carefully traced jack-o-lanterns leering from grade school windows. But they arrived only after colored leaves drizzled across the East Tennessee hillsides of my childhood. Remaining taped there, fading a little where the sun found them, the pumpkins provided a backdrop for fierce third-grade Indians and snaggle-toothed Pilgrims. Not until the Monday following an overstuffed Thanksgiving did we remove our brittle artwork, and then only to make room for plump snowmen and Christmas stars.

My decades of blustery autumns and enchanted yuletides collide with today's clustered holidays.

Somewhere we've misplaced the fun of drawing out the moment, of savoring the waiting. Time has become compressed until, in an instant-replay view of life, we hustle to anticipate the next move in life's games, afraid to more than glance at present action.

During the weekend housecleaning, I thumbed through a popular Christmas wish book already dog-eared with dreams, lists peeking from between its tempting pages. Hints are passed casually around the family table before frost has nipped the pumpkins on the backyard fence. But I resist it all, unwilling to include these suggestions in my shopping lists.

I know, I know . . . it would be economical and efficient to add myself to the flock of early-bird shoppers. But I need to catch a few snowflakes on the tip of my tongue and burn a cord of wood before 'twill be my season to be jolly. Mood and atmosphere are essential for savoring turned calendar pages.

Some things never change, though, despite our accelerated seasonal revolutions.

Contents of last night's bulging trick-or-treat sacks, still considered high stakes, are heaped on our kitchen table. Bargaining and swapping continue through the generations as squashed candy bars are traded for bubble gum. The black jelly beans are left to harden on the counter.

Soon the day of the turkey will be upon us. Our Miles Standish and Priscilla Alden candles will be briefly united across the brass fruit bowl. My husband will retrieve the roaster from the highest pantry shelf, and we'll fill cornucopias with our annual thankfulness.

And then, only then, can I change my personal season's color from fall's cozy, musty hues to bustling, merry shades of red and green.

Season's Greetings.

Prayer

I always feel behind, Lord, even when I'm not. It's the pace of things, life all scrunched together, life at a glance with no chance to enjoy the present.

Our seasons blend unsavored, Lord.

We worry about putting Junior through college before he's born; our retirement looms on the horizon before a gray hair sprouts. Too much too soon and all together.

Help us sort out what today is and let tomorrow follow as it will. And give us the courage to ignore bathing suits in December, school clothes and book bags in July, and college in maternity.

Restore our common sense. Let us not be shuffled like cattle down the right aisle to consume this month's inventory before it's time.

To everything there is a season, a time, and it's now: not tomorrow, but today. Unwind our foolish commercial clocks to the real time.

Pull us from the fast lane where we are speeding past the day's joys, the moment's magic because we're afraid we might miss the preholiday sale, the preseason bargain. Help us check the inventory of our own needs, stocking up only on what we need, not what we're told we do.

Protect us, the consumers, Lord, lest we hastily gulp something not good for us. Rid us of our frantic fear that "it might be gone" if we don't get it ahead of time. Yes, Lord, the thing that might be gone is today and its fullness thereof.

4

Doll Clothes

Winter came early that year. Arriving impatiently in a gale of sleet and snow, it closed roads and schools one early December day.

The children, delighted with a holiday, ventured outside. Lugging sleds behind them, they left me free to begin Christmas baking.

Soon, a snowball exploding against the kitchen window signaled their return. Wiping a clear patch on the frosty windowpane with a towel, I watched as they trudged across the road from Grandma's house.

Sighing, I shook flour from my hands. How I wished it were as easy to be rid of the burden covering me and the children, the sixth generation to live on the family farm. Already they were showing the same strong ancestral spirit that had tamed prairie lands more than a century ago. Schools, farms, and churches had been built then, and the family name was chiseled on numerous cornerstones.

Now garlands of family customs encircled our lives with single-minded merriment as descendants gathered each Christmas in the central homestead, "The Colony." Even I bowed to family, I fumed, stirring the ginger-cookie batter with more than necessary vigor, eggs and

27

sugar splattering. And as yet another yuletide approached, I yearned for freedom.

Visions of Aunty's pumpkin pie served from its traditional spot on the crowded oak table mocked me. Extended across Grandma's dining room, its legacy of spills and family toasts had silenced me for the nine years I'd sat on the right corner next to the rolls.

"I simply can't face another year," I wailed to Catherine, a friend from a nearby town.

What if? we wondered. What if we were in charge, what then?

Swirling tea leaves drying in my mug, I agreed. "Let's do it." Soon plans were completed for making a new tradition joining our two families in Christmas celebration. Fearfully determined and with curiously lifted spirits, we parted, eager to share our plan.

Driving carefully home on snow-packed roads, I wondered what to give this special friend. Transplanted also by marriage to different customs and climate, Catherine was an outsider here, too, and understood my timid rebellion against traditions.

She'd borne only sons and always welcomed my five-year-old Lynn, a cherished borrowed daughter. They held elaborate tea parties, drinking from fragile cups, and Lynn never had to eat the bread crust on sandwiches when visiting "Aunt" Catherine.

Perhaps a gift to please both.

A doll and clothes, I thought suddenly while picking up toys later that day. Bedtime rituals completed, I retrieved scraps from Lynn's dresses from the bottom of my sewing trunk.

During the following days, details were arranged, the menu planned, groceries bought, the ancestors' wrath endured.

I bought a doll and secretly fashioned tiny clothes, copying patterns from the child's wardrobe, including a miniature pink silk flower girl's dress from a recent wedding and a wisp of a hat.

Christmas Day.

Laden with packages and food, we traipsed through freshly fallen snow to Catherine's fragrant kitchen and blazing hearth. The goose was golden and mild, the rum pudding exceptionally smooth and creamy.

The table was cleared at last, the dishes done, and we gathered around the shimmering tree. Squirming in excitement, Lynn carried their big silver package to Catherine.

Together they discovered the doll and her tiny wardrobe, their delight reflected in the Christmas lights mirrored on frosty panes. Enchanted, they dressed the patient doll in a mellow Christmas afterglow.

Later, we toasted our friendship and offered a prayer of thanks for new traditions to celebrate the oldest one. A good day, we agreed. Certainly a tradition worth repeating.

The months passed in a glare of icy roads and sudden spring thunderstorms. And again Lynn was taking Catherine a gift.

I watched as she scuffed across the dry, brittle July grass carrying the gift to her friend. A heavy clay pot, it was filled with the exuberantly blooming yellow weeds Lynn had carefully transplanted from the field. Gingerly, she placed it upon a fresh mound of dirt among the withering bouquets on the grave.

Victim of a sudden illness, Catherine left behind a life scarcely more than begun.

"I know she would've liked my pretty yellow flowers," the somber child assured me as we trudged away from this last journey of friendship.

Christmases have come and gone, the restlessness never nagging me again. We returned to the family table, content to admire the newest baby and nibble pumpkin pie. And, in time, the children and I made our way to other tables, new traditions and families.

Balancing precariously on the edge of a chair yesterday, I lifted the dusty box from the closet shelf into waiting hands of the grown children home for the holidays. I carried the faded silver box and placed it beneath the freshly cut tree already glorious with paper chains and homemade ornaments.

Sitting beneath its fragrance, we unpacked the silver box, its faded contents restored to grandeur in the twinkling, starry lights. Rousing the loveworn doll from slumber amidst her delicate wardrobe, I put her in the place of honor, an antique cradle.

Tired, I soon headed upstairs for bed. Glancing back, I watched as Lynn knelt for a moment to rearrange the doll. Tying the straw bonnet more securely beneath the doll's chin, she straightened a fragile yellow flower and tucked it behind a frayed blue velvet ribbon encircling the brim.

Plucked from that long ago summer's gift, it reminds us that some of the best traditions are those dared to be broken. Splintering into shards of memory, each fragment reflects prisms of friendship grown more brilliant with time's passage.

Prayer

The holidays can be the worst, Lord, especially the one when we're supposed to be celebrating your birth. But what we really do is bind one another in traditions and hollow rituals that threaten to smother us.

We worship sameness, the predictable gestures and habits. But, Lord, there often stirs in me a determination to be about something new, a chance to find out what this season of love is calling to me, the gifts it offers.

Forgive me, Lord, if I'm absent from the family table or where I usually am. But I think you can be found in other places and times, too.

Forgive my rebellious heart, my childish foot stomping.

But give me the courage to venture, to explore, to answer the little voice that whispers, "Go ahead."

And if that is not you, Lord, beckoning me, forgive.

Roots

Pewter-colored clouds somersaulted across the spring sky, chased by a heavy air mass shooing them along. Gusts tugged me in a zigzag path as the old collie and I fled to the house from the mailbox.

Minutes later, we watched through the parlor window as a tornado tore through our farmstead like a teenager in search of something to wear, tossing things helter-skelter.

Timbers from the century-old barn were flung, javelins in the hand of the storm, through the sides of a nearby shed; roofs were peeled away from rafters, exposing startled livestock to the deluge that washed fresh seeds from their rows and topsoil into ditches.

At the house, a sixty-foot cedar tree was wrenched from the front yard and flung at the window that framed me and the dog, too frightened to move.

The first casualty I inspected after the storm had had its way with us was the tree, twisted corkscrew fashion from the ground. The size and depth of its exposed, broken roots told just how deeply they'd buried themselves, enabling the tree to shade generations sitting in this parlor and to withstand dust storms, drought, and prairie winds. Yanked rudely from their source of life, they could no longer feed and support the tree despite our repair efforts, and it died before there were new shingles on the barn roof.

Seasons later, having moved from there twice before coming to my current home, I tentatively yank on my own roots. I wonder just how deeply they're buried. I've lived in this state half of my life, and now I'm moving from it.

Here, my roots are grown deep and intertwined with others. Friendships and shared experiences nourished them; raising three young children sent them ever-deeper; divorce urged them still deeper searching for bedrock upon which to rest and for a spring to provide water during dry seasons ahead.

Now it's time to move on to a new state, a new home. A new marriage begun with the spring is a fitting time for beginnings, we agree, as we exchange rings.

My roots quiver and resist, though, as our new life tugs them. I don't want to move and I squat like a homesteader on my claim.

Yet, we must continue to gather information on possible new locations, exchanging histories with prospective employers. Schools, doctors, property tax rates, and pollution indexes are evaluated, and my firm grasp on familiar territory is lessened with each letter, each phone call.

Cobwebs on the ceiling, hanging like laundry from the line, mock me as I drink my early morning tea before the rest of the family stirs. Why clean the windows or shampoo the carpet? Why renew magazine subscriptions, my library card?

Listless, I hold life at arm's length, afraid to let go of the old and unsure of the new. Jealously, I hoard each today, even finding pleasure in our hideous green house, as familiar and dear as the freckle on my chin.

Of no help at all, interstate introductions to new communities leave me with lasting first impressions.

Two grimy-necked children stop traffic as they drag dilapidated tricycles from their junk- and mongrel-filled yard to the other side of the railroad track. How conveniently their poverty erases from my mind thoughts of raises, more bathrooms, and new opportunities that might exist here.

Another day, we hurriedly close air vents and raise car windows to seal off the alarmingly caustic factory fumes greeting us at this town's main entrance. Do people here hang out their sheets? Do they plant gardens, let their children out of the air-conditioned safety of their houses? Of course not, I assume, peacock proud of my clean air back home.

Houses in a subdivision smartly salute us like soldiers on parade, alike in their neatly arranged ranks—grey shutters here, red there being the only observable differences on another foray into possibilities. I smirk at the individuality I've stamped even on our acidic green house.

Another day, another town, I am hemmed in and trapped under the television antennas hovering over the whole area like an aluminum mesh hairnet. Could I ever adjust to or learn to tolerate having my days punctuated with the arrivals and departures of jets landing at this town's international airport? Never.

From behind carefully arranged casualness, golf club estates on the edge of yet another prospective town note the make of our car, the labels in our clothes, the degrees on our wall. Will my jeans and hiking boots get me past the mock-colonial pillars? Could I refinish my old meal bin in the backyard? Is a fort built by small boys on Saturday afternoons an appropriate lawn decoration?

Is there nowhere to belong? I cry, my tears puddling on the road map I wad into unrecognizable creases like the traffic lanes surrounding us.

I just want to go home. Wherever that is.

And once I get there, I vow, I will never, ever put down any more roots. Mrs., Ms., Mobile American, that's me, able to roam the country collecting jobs and towns like decals on a camper window. No more of this wrenching pain at pulling up my roots like that poor destroyed tree, so I'll put none down. I'm footloose and fancy free, unfettered, uprooted.

And yet, was the tree wasted?

I am left wondering this by a picture of dear friends tucked into a box of photographs I'm packing to take with us to our new town. From the tree's leftovers came a bonfire the autumn following the tornado, smooth pieces of incense for blanket chests, a carved letter opener. In the photograph, I'm with these friends popping corn in their fireplace, which blazes with the tree's logs.

Holding up the photograph and looking once again into the flames and the tree as it had been, beginnings and endings turn to embers, and its roots nudge me. They're still prodding me as the moving van backs into the driveway, and I think about the woman I met several weeks ago when I was house hunting in our new town. We'd had iced tea together and a conversation full of promise for a place to set down roots next to her warmth. I found the library on the first visit, an antique shop and ice cream store the second. Tomorrow when we get there, I'm hunting for the pizza places, a staple in our home.

Home. The word rolls around on my tongue like bubble gum not yet softened, and I savor its newness.

I brake at the intersection, the moving van already two blocks ahead of me, before pulling onto the interstate. Signaling left, I wind down the ramp and onto the route home, uprooted but struggling to grow, not wither and die.

Prayer

A stick-in-the-mud, Lord, that's what I am. A tree-in-the-mud, really, for my roots burrow deeply into places I indelibly brand "home sweet home." Yet, how many change-of-address labels will I have to fill out in my lifetime? How many times will I have to repaint my color schemes over someone else's tastes?

How can I not suffer so during the in-between times when I dramatize moving as if it's penalty instead of possibility? No one would ever know I carry pioneer blood in my veins, Lord, covered-wagon stock. A pitiful heir.

Another contradiction is a favorite antique walnut rope bed. Rope, Lord, do you know why it's assembled with ropes lashed end-to-end instead of with hardware? So it could be easily dismantled, loaded, and trundled across the country in a covered wagon. Go on without me, I holler; I want my beds bolted to the floor.

If I shouldn't yearn for such needlessly tenacious roots as my cedar tree, Lord, then I don't want them to be like the superficial locust trees that grow thick in our woods, either. Growing close to the surface, their roots do little more than steady the trees long enough for a brisk wind to come along. Down they go, toppled over in the winds of change, leaning dangerously drunk against one another, their skimpy roots hanging flat-footed out of the soil.

But save me from stagnation at the same time you protect me from shallowness. It's deadly, Lord, I know, for I've killed many of my plants with too much water and too small containers.

Thank you for the lesson my plants provide me, Lord, in their yellow leaves and droopy foliage while they are adjusting to new pots (when I think to provide them). Give me the assurance that I, too, will stretch tall again and send out tentative new shoots wherever I am planted.

Forgive my reluctance, my lack of vision, my rejection of new homes sight unseen. Pardon my clinging worship of the old, the comfortable, and the familiar. I root-bind myself in my hand-wringing worries that there is only one place—the place I happen to be at the time—to call home.

Too, Lord, restrain me from chasing after elusive promises of greener pastures in the backyards of new homes, promises that are always heralded by that great word *if.* If I move, then. Fill in the blanks, Lord, with whatever is the solution I think to find by running away. For, like turtles, we carry home around with us, and there is no new home that can long distract our attention from problems that invariably come home to roost.

Teach me the wisdom to know when to stay and when to go, for moving is not always progress any more than staying is always stagnating.

A riddle for your mobile children; for your stuck-in-the-mud ones, too.

The Vote

The vote was split on whether I should've come to the wedding. Especially late.

An informal poll rippled through the congregation in an averted glance, a surprised smile, an indrawn breath, as I was ushered to my pew a dignified distance behind my ex-husband and his new family.

Did the six rows separating us make a mockery of the solemn vows about to be repeated, the hopes and promises sealed with a pastoral benediction?

Did my presence remind those gathered that marriages are neither made nor lived in heaven, that divorce interrupts at least half the marriages begun in such promise as this? But perhaps this marriage will last, avoiding chasms of change too deep to be renegotiated.

A perfect wedding, perfect bride, perfect punch —such unblemished perfection is surely too fragile to sustain marriage circa the 1980s. Yet I, too, joined in wishing them well, offering congratulations for at least making the effort. Kissing the young bride, daughter of a dear friend, on her radiant cheek, I offered my silent prayer that she succeed where others, including me, falter, if not fail. For no matter how much better the future looks than the past, divorce's division remains painful, the taste of failure unpalatable.

Gentle breezes teased violet satin bows and lacy, virginal tablecloths as I strolled the garden reception playing at remembering when. I left my beribboned gift with the others, a photograph album to preserve commitments captured between pages of possibilities, lest they become brittle and dusty with time.

Struggling to remember names and connections with fellow guests, I was shocked at the untimely death of a friend's forty-year-old husband. A double loss, for I had not known, having lost my place of comfort at her side.

An empty chair beside another was a welcome extended to me by an old friend of a decade ago. From others came an unspoken challenge, their eyes chanting, "Red Rover . . . we dare you to come over."

But come over I had, traveling for many hours on once-familiar highways, unsure if I wanted landmarks the same or very different, as if I'd never known them.

Many were bulldozed beyond memory's reach, but some were still present: a single gnarled apple tree, remnant of a neighbor's orchard; the old schoolyard with the same swing set. No cows grazed nearby. No dairy barns stood where now only a windmill, disconnected from its pump and turning haphazardly in the breeze, reminded of the swath progress can cut.

Faintly visible, too, was a grassy lane leading to what had once been a dignified farmstead. In that yard grew the hickory trees where my children and I had gathered nuts each fall, our autumnal rite of passage. Nothing there now, not even mocking ghosts at curtainless windows.

The formal invitation had come a month before, its engraved message my passport down the rabbit hole of what once was, before divorce rerouted our lives.

Ten years' absence is just long enough before returning, a decade when some wounds heal, others fester. For me, intercepting a kaleidoscope of glances in the gaily chattering crowd, it was picking at an old scab grown tough and thick on an old sore.

Issues long grown irrelevant to my new life were being raised again by those who'd had to hate the old before loving the new, the second wife, who had successfully rousted me from a marriage approaching a dangerous comfortableness. Irresistible with her promise of wildflower springs in the nearing midwinters of a tired husband's life, she'd called my bluff. For a moment, I allowed myself a blaze of white-hot fury, rekindled in my discomfort at being an alien in her territory where I had reigned so long.

Yet, watching and listening to this small-town chatter, it was as if I'd never been gone. I could still finish sentences only half begun, and anticipate the see-saw dialogue of a couple who never agreed. The familiarity tumbled me into a time warp suddenly uncomfortable, into what had once been pinching like too-tight shoes. The invitation: my ticket in. The divorce: my ticket out. With a farewell hug for my friend and her beautiful bride, I fled to my sweltering car, glad to escape down hot, dusty roads lined with corn rows, narrow and even like the lives they enclosed.

Prayer

I never meant to be a failure, Lord, never meant to break commitments I'd made so solemnly. But I am and I did. And I mourn the loss of innocence that crumbled beneath the knowledge that I couldn't be who I needed to be and stay in that marriage.

Comfort those of us who make the hard decisions—whether to stay or go—in marriages that are not good; that are hurtful in little or big ways; that are tightly stoppered with no room in which to grow; that are missing your leavening, your framework, and your guidance.

Comfort those of us who mourn the loss of friendships and landmarks left behind, a hidden cost in divorce's settlement of who gets what, silverware to bridge partners. Guide our steps away from where we must leave toward where we can go to other friends, other landmarks.

But, dear Lord, keep us from doing this casually. Deafen our modern ears to boasts that divorce is no more painful than clipping one's nails. Steel our resolves against accepting easy ways out of even the worst marriages; too many find another just like it to slip back into, never missing a beat in the rhythm of marriage. Grant us wisdom to not repeat mistakes, to do better the next time if there's no other way.

Forgive those who must still hate the old before they can love the new. I struggle to forgive, but I often get stuck trying to prove why they shouldn't. Help me to let them be.

Thank you for your powerful grace that douses the stubborn embers of bitterness and rejection that threaten any new loves with their burning, consuming energy.

So, be with me, Lord, as I once again leave a place and people loved and known as my own. Be with me as I stand, amazed at how easily I was replaced. Hold up to me your vision of me so that I will not believe I am no more important than a bit player in a well-performed farce.

Be with me, Lord, on my way home; the trip has never seemed longer.

7

Three "R's"

Familiar smells of chalkdust, disinfectant, and food greeted me as I pulled open the heavy doors. The sour aftertaste of breakfast and a dull pain just below my ribs signaled the arrival of school stomachache.

First day of school.

My uneasiness increased when I saw only boys standing beside the nearby water fountain. I had probably come in the wrong door. What luck.

Which way to go now?

Two wrong turns led me past a group of giggling girls, matched sets in their carefully arranged casualness. Glad not to be a part of a bunch like that. Who'd want to hear any of their dumb old secrets anyhow? I stalked on past, hoping I wouldn't blunder into a storeroom, yet unwilling to ask directions. With a shared glance of dismissal toward me, they turned back to their chatter, and I wandered out of earshot.

Determined wanderings eventually led me to the office. The clock's unsmiling face scolded, reminding me that I was late. My clenched jaw ached; my eyes were gritty with unshed tears.

Borrowing a pencil, I filled in the blanks, stumbling

over my new address and making erasures. Why did I have to go to school anyway? I just wanted to go home.

When I eventually found and entered the classroom, conversation stopped. Lost again, I was late for class. All heads turned toward my direction as the students took roll.

The whispered query, "Is this our teacher?" ricocheted through the room while I made my way to the remaining seat. Aloof, I scrutinized my desk, relieved when the "real" teacher arrived.

Relief was premature, however, I realized when the test booklets were distributed. Unfamiliar words, lengthy instructions, and ominous time limits returned my uncomprehending stares. Examples blurred before my eyes. Frantically I searched back nearly twenty years for an "elliptical expression." Verbs refused to be conjugated, participles dangled before me, and multiple choices sang a rhythmic trio as backup to my headache.

Calm down, concentrate, try again, ignore the other students casually completing and turning pages while I'm barely halfway down the first, I advised myself.

Mental reflexes had definitely stiffened, if not atrophied, over the two decades since last I'd occupied a desk-with-an-attached-arm for reasons other than parents' visiting day at my children's schools.

I was a midthirties outsider in the late-teen environment of English 109 at a junior college, a piccolo in a tuba section. Just beginning to trickle back into matriculation, we "mature" students had discovered that college was an essential detour to take on the way out of low-paying jobs, inertia, or sudden lifestyle changes such as divorce or empty nests. Many, mothers and housewives, wanted to rearrange and update lives molded by routine to fit the shapeless, well-worn chenille robes they kept on until after the second cup of morning coffee.

Whatever the reasons we'd driven out of our driveways this morning to become students, we were all rusty. Yet, despite the clever way younger minds had tucked them out of easy access, I found my other classrooms during the day.

In the process, I picked up a returning sense of curiosity—that speck under the eyelash that had prodded me from hearth and home to books and thoughts, to stretching mind, so I could pursue a postponed literary itch and transfer it from fleeting thought to scribbled deed.

A bookstore's lure is equally strong with its bright book jackets, inviting and provocative titles. New authors, new topics, new vocabulary. Heady reading, and I spent my lunch hour soaking up academia from its shelves.

Finally, as proud as any first grader, I lugged my newly purchased texts and virginal notebooks—tickets of admission to this new reel of my life—from class to class. Unthinkable to stash any of them in a locker; I'd waited a long time to have this particular backache.

A navy blue T-shirt emblazoned with the college seal bought at the last minute slipped easily over my sensible blouse. Now I belonged. Now I was one with those who wandered with me through the puzzling corridors, and I exchanged hearty greetings with the sprinkling of other adults, waving like cousins at a reunion.

The younger students helped, advised, and asked. Mostly asked. Why, they wondered, would I come to school? Many of them were there because parents had forced them, they said, bewildered at the sight of a parent-classmate. What had I left behind? What did I hope to take back with me? Did I have change for the telephone?

Typical student talk, I thought gleefully. And I was speaking it.

Weak from struggling with blanks, essays, and multiple choices, I finally fled to my car, one of the more sedate in the lot, temporarily lost, of course, in the parking maze. What better climax for Mom's first day of school.

Exhausted, I arrived home to the waiting family. Clutching to my withered mind and body, I had a "show and tell," I announced to the impressed group who had supper waiting. A compliment, it had been bestowed upon me by a fellow student, albeit young, between qualifying exams, "If you didn't talk about your husband and kids, no one would know for sure you really *are* old."

Awesome, as we students say. An awesome day.

Prayer

O Lord, I did it! I made it through my first day at school. I can feel my mind stretching, opening up like hands to take what is there just for the asking.

Thank you for my hunger, my restlessness, gifts from you I've complained about before. I know, I know, without them I would be content to stagnate, stew, and settle for being less than I can be. Less than you must think I can be, too, otherwise why would you go with me?

Didn't you marvel at it all today, as we moved along corridors flowing with people dressed and talking in ways that must baffle even you? They were beautiful, weren't they? A flower garden, grown leggy and a bit wild perhaps, like roses left unpruned, but beautiful.

And we had quite a day, didn't we? Surprises and beginnings may not be so awesome to you, author of them all as you are, but for me, I hardly know where to begin in this new venture.

At the beginning? Not an answer I want to hear, Lord. Impatient, impatient, foot-stomping impatient, I want to be moving, flying, soaring above the mediocrity that's tethered me till now. I want to make up for my late start, my hesitations and stallings.

At the beginning, you still insist?

Let me apply my new-found knowledge to this question. I wonder if the answer you want me to discover isn't a day-by-day one, an answer that will lead me gently through so many choices I am dizzy thinking of them, so that I can make sure it's the one you need me to know. At the beginning, then, Lord, it will be.

A question for you, then, Lord: if I'm not who I was, nor who I am yet to be, who am I today at this beginning?

A hungry child.

Yes, Lord, that is the right answer. A hungry child who thanks you for a myriad of questions to explore. Thank you for second, third chances, for beginnings, for firsts, for perplexing questions. Keep me from easy answers and quick answers.

And now I must do my homework, an essay on what I want to be when I grow up! Yes, we already know the answer: a hungry child.

Awesome.

With This Ring

Fresh ideas for an article I am writing on marriage are as elusive as grains of sand in a sieve. Doodling in the margins of imagination, I conjure up a television game show, "Marriage Wheel of Chance," with lots of prizes behind velvet curtains for the lucky winners to spin and win.

Hurrah! I realize I've got the contestants in my file.

Meet Mr. and Mrs. Couple A. They're together once a month: they have a commuter marriage two states apart.

Next, meet Mr. and Mrs. Couple B. They're together every day, as they have been for seventy-five years: they have a stay-at-home marriage.

Which couple has the greatest odds of winning the grand prize behind the curtain? What is that prize? How do you get it instead of what 2.3 million get each year: divorces?

I sign myself out of the newsroom to hunt for answers.

For these, Couple A, understandably, was not available to interview. Maybe next month, they guessed, and I'd settled for letters and a wish for luck to these marital pioneers.

After several delays, I'd finally set up an appointment with Couple B, today's destination, a week before their wedding anniversary to celebrate being married three-quarters of a century.

How? I ask later, curiosity and pencil poised from my comfortable spot on their couch.

They look at each other as if to find the answer written between the lines on the other's face. "A day at a time," they suggest lamely.

"Get used to being henpecked," he adds, dodging the hand she sends flying his way along with a chuckle, her answer. "Without a sense of humor, no one can make it," she says, and I take diligent professional notes.

Some of the years have been happy, they tell me, speaking slowly so that I can get it right on my tablet. Some of the other years, they say, have been a mite "tetchy."

"Tetchy?"

Is that what you call it, I wonder, embarrassed to ask if my own marital frustrations qualify as "tetchy."

"Sure," they say.

Being a mite "tetchy" can grow, they warn, though, into the sulks. Next thing you know, it's a feud, they predict, nodding at one another in recollection of a few that were, they confess, "dillies."

"Making up is worth it," they continue. Present tense: is.

"But you have to be around one another to make up," they say, glad they avoided taking separate paths as do today's couples.

I don't even mention the commuter couple, having no words in my handy pocket dictionary to link together a sensible sentence of explanation.

Postscript, though, they add: couples should include two independent people. Different interests, jobs, hobbies, and even personalities only serve to sweeten the marriage pie, they promise.

Surreptitiously, I turn to the blank back page of my reporter's notebook to start a list of my own. Although lame, a bit deaf, and seeing through pop-bottle thick lenses, these ninety-plus-year-old sweethearts are still way ahead of my understanding of marriage.

"Dear husband," I write first, surprised at what the pencil makes of this afternoon. I'd thought to write great words of wisdom.

"Dear husband?" A greeting? for how often do I say something so nice first? A declaration of fact? for he is dear. An aggravated sigh, as in Oh, dear? for he is an aggravation.

Dear. Hold that thought, I tell myself, flipping back to the interview's pages.

Next, add hard work to the list of secrets to married bliss, they advise. Both worked outside the home he built from timbers on their land, adding on rooms for the children they both parented. They laugh at my new word for what they did: a verb where it used to be just a noun. A proud noun.

They worked inside the house together, too. Before the visit is over, he will roll up his sleeves and do the dishes we dirty together. If it needs to be done, do it, they say, not needing a duty roster on the fridge to tell whose turn it is.

In these less hectic twilight years, they share still more tasks, even the laundry, and I take out my camera for this: one cranks the wringer, the other catches the clothes to hang on the line. "When the weather is good," they say, laughing out loud at my confusion.

I don't understand their laughter until I see the brand new washer-dryer combo hiding in the background. When the weather is bad, or they're tired, they confess, they do automatic washing. A snapshot of them advances my film: a portrait of equal rights unlike any posters I have proudly tacked on my office wall.

And when her cookie-batter stirring arm was recovering from a break, he was right there with a spoon, they add, tickled to be helping me so much with my story.

Togetherness, I write on my back page.

"But isn't too much togetherness dangerous?" I ask. "Doesn't it limit each person and make for boring the other?"

When he's boring, she confides behind a raised hand just loud enough for him to hear, she turns off her hearing aid and just smiles and nods. He joins in her joke, and I sit shaking my head.

The together times are the rewards, they try to explain, rewards for the rigors of their separate days, the on-the-job stresses and at-home pressures with kids underfoot early on; later, from grandkids; still later, from an adult widowed child home for a while.

I picture them escaping into an interlude over the washer—the old one, not the new—talking, sharing as they push and pull the steaming clothes.

Faith, they announce, afraid I'd missed their obvious center.

"Right over there," she points, "is where the minister sits when he comes to dinner." No longer choir members or teachers, they must content themselves with being pillars of a church where they will celebrate their anniversary Sunday in a recommitment of vows.

Commitment. Recommitment, I hastily write next on my back-page blueprint.

To the world, too, they clarify, after God and to one another. For if you're not committed to your world, it will drive your crazy. And they should know, having lived a history-book panorama of cars, electricity, telephones, wars, moon walks, and two sightings of Halley's Comet.

Adaptability, I abbreviate, not wanting to miss a word in the tales they tell so easily, passing conversation like a weaver's shuttle back and forth.

Absentee ballots in this election year take care of a pledge to the world. Relatives take care of them when illness intrudes.

We'd had to postpone this visit for several weeks due to one of those illnesses, and I'd crossed Couple B off my list of possible story subjects along with Couple A. But when they called to reschedule, she gave me directions to their house, not a daughter's.

It was nice, they acknowledged, to not have to worry about hot meals, or laundry, while they were gone. But it just wasn't the same. So he proposed again. "Let's go home," he said.

"And that's where we'll be," they say. Wrapping his arms around her at the front door as I finally tear myself away, he lets out a dramatic sigh, guessing, he says, that he might as well stay with her at this point.

In my rearview mirror I can see they hold hands and they watch me as I go down the gravel drive.

Prayer

He tracked sawdust from his woodworking shop into the clean kitchen again tonight, Lord. And I yelled. Something rude but justified, because I'd just vacuumed and dusted. Once or twice a month, Lord, that's all I ask for a clean house. Is that too much?

So I yelled about the telltale prints following themselves in and out as he rummaged for a stain-mixing jar. He apologized, adding that he'd forgotten to remove his shoes and sawdusty coveralls.

Again, I point out to his retreating back.

Does he feel that I think of him as dear? I suddenly wonder, recalling my back-page notes. Does he know that I treasure him as my best friend? Does he believe my commitment is as certain as tides and time? Does he understand I'm proud of him, button-popping proud? Of so many things, but especially the furniture he builds in his spare time.

If so, Lord, I confess as I reread today's interview notes, it is because he has faith in me. Faith, but not a lot of evidence.

"Dear husband," I wrote.

Such a gap between my words and actions, and I cringe at the gaps I leave for the unwary to fall headlong into. Gaps, Lord, I suddenly see, that can only widen under the prying jaws of my daily frustrations that don't all belong to this dear man. I send him the bill for them anyhow.

This husband. This maker of sawdust, which is what he jokes he makes in his workshop, a place I wish he had more time to enjoy. When was the last time I said that? Tonight, I'll say it tonight.

You know how carpenters are, Lord, those dusty folks who take planks and make tables; boards and make houses; sawdust and make marriages and families.

For from sawdust—walnut, cherry, oak, poplar, curly maple—this dear husband has created doll cradles, rocking horses, cupboards, cabinets, a desk with a secret drawer for those of us fortunate to become his new family a baker's dozen years ago.

I brought the kids, Lord, an instant family; he provided sawdust from which to surround us in his steadfast love. Not complaining, either, about how a family now takes time from the shop; how braces, tennis shoes, and colleges deplete sugar bowl savings for lumber.

Bless this sawdust, Lord, that I am wiping up, down on my hands and knees. Silence my words and smooth my frowning face at the footprints he sometimes forgets and traipses across my path.

O Lord, give me years with this dear husband so that I can learn how to piece together your gift, a counterpane of married love. We won't have seventy-five years, Lord, for we got a late start, but I thank you for my being with him at all.

Let me gently pluck the shavings from his hair, the splinters from his thumb. Let me see his sawdust for what it is: evidence of love sprinkled like fingerprint powder over our lives that, like the kitchen, proudly bear his mark.

It's nearly midnight, Lord, too late for him to worry about cleaning up his mess I'd assured him would be waiting. I hollered out to the shop, offering to clean it up, and am indicted by his pleased surprise. Let it not be so long before I offer something again.

Almost done, Lord, with this mess, when I see a chance as if it's been blown here on purpose.

I draw a heart ("I love you," it says) in the feathery sawdust that's sifted onto even the kitchen table. Let him see it, Lord. I promise to quit being in such a hurry to sweep up its message.

9

Gift of Love

Some day off, I sighed.

Notes overflowed my desk, greasy dishes stuck to the kitchen counter, and I'd yet to sit down on my one Saturday off this month.

Late as usual, I parked behind the church and scurried inside. The basement echoed with silent laughter as a circus-poster-come-alive greeted me with waves and exaggerated bows. Our high school clown troupe and I had a date.

Quickly, I smeared white makeup across my scowling face, around tired eyes and tight mouth.

Why do you do this? my reflection questioned in the dusty mirror. Does it really matter? Wouldn't bake sales and car washes make more sense?

A generous sprinkling of baby powder followed by a quick swipe with a wet sponge set my white face, soft now and dry to the touch and not nearly so grim. My "Pinky" clown had been born.

I climbed into oversized clothes and with a final flourish drew a bright red smile and astonished yellow eyebrows. A green dot on my left cheek marked the special ministry of a clown.

"Some ministry," I muttered.

Straightening my wig of springy pink curls, I switched off the lights and left the room still cloudy with powder.

Mute, for clowns don't speak, we clambered aboard the van, brimming with balloons, for a trip to a nearby major city. The young clowns waved at surprised fellow travelers along the highway and practiced bending and twisting shiny balloons into parrots, dogs, and fat red apples.

Separated from reality by our white faces, we parked and entered a large hospital complex, a place where most of us would be unwilling, uncomfortable visitors. Waiting elevators whisked us upward to a place where laughter seldom visited, where smiles too often seemed as painted on as ours.

I wondered who waited, and if we were ready.

The whispered closing of our elevator doors wakened a young man two doors down the hall. He kept his eyes closed against the pale spring sun slipping around the curtains.

If he were home, he'd probably be down at the river to see if the fish were running. And, if he were lucky, he'd take a string of fish home for his mom to fix for supper.

Home. Slowly, savoring each thought, his memory walked from room to room checking details as he'd last seen them. Smells and sounds tumbled through his mind, and he breathed deeply as memory entered the room he shared with a younger brother. Sweaty smells from their basketball clothes lying on the floor mixed with the stinging odor of turpentine he used in his painting. Their dog, Ginger, and her musky smell drifted to him as she stretched in her sleep atop his rumpled lower bunk bed. His hand flexed, and he could feel the rough yet silky texture of her golden fur beneath his fingers, her snores under his palm.

But his hand couldn't move very far without encountering the edge of his bed. The needle taped to his arm anchored him to this place where no muddy animals belonged, where the only smells stung with antiseptic and frightening pungency.

Few of his friends came anymore. Their words were unable to wind through the maze of tubes and bottles defining the margins of his dwindling life. No stereos sang their ballads of youth and adventure for him.

Most of the time now, though, he was content to enjoy the silence. He had accepted, finally, that he was to be his only companion on the last journey of his seventeen years. And, as much as he could, he tried to ease the good-byes whispering from the eyes of those who continued to sit by him.

His recollections were interrupted by sounds of hesitantly shuffling feet. Before he opened his eyes, he tried to guess who it would be. It didn't feel like time for either more medicine or visitors. And few strangers entered this quiet room. In a life that is ending, there is often not room for much new.

Curiosity, an unfamiliar feeling for him lately, fluttered in his mind, and he quickly opened his eyes.

A clown.

An unplanned surprise spread across his face. Giggles astonished the still hospital room as another clown and I tiptoed to his bedside. "Pinky's" composure carefully hid my anguish at the sight of his wasted body pinned to the bed by tubes and machines.

Probably just a few weeks left, the nurse had explained. And so lonely.

Slowly I fished a bright blue balloon from my cavernous pocket. Gathering an outlandishly huge breath of air, I huffed and puffed in the elaborate task of inflating it.

Intrigued, the young man watched as it slowly swelled. Knotting it, I carefully attached it to his IV pole.

"Love" was emblazoned in flowery script on both sides. For a moment, it reflected my no-longer-painted-on smile as I leaned over and softly touched his gaunt hand.

Surprise—and laughter, its partner—shuffled from the room as silently as they'd arrived. Closing the door behind me, I leaned for a moment against the corridor wall.

Some ministry.

It was time for us to leave. Another day, another attempt, and now back home.

The young man dozed for a while, swept upward on wings of pain and fatigue. He wondered when he awoke if the clowns had been part of a dream scurrying through his drowsy thoughts. A smile played once again on his lips, though, as he opened one eye and saw the bright blue message left behind by his visitor.

Even here in life's last efforts, there was still room for something new, he decided.

He could hardly wait to see the expressions on his family's tired, strained faces when they saw the balloon—a gift to take with him on this last journey, a companion of love.

Prayer

I'm too old for this foolishness, Lord. An hour to get ready, twice that to scrub my face clean. But I have to admit that I become the new creation you promised from behind my white face.

I can, in my silence, hear what the lonely, hurting, fragile, and afraid are saying. And, too, when I'm not so busy talking, I can hear you.

Bless my clown, Lord. It is the servant part of me, the pretense and phoniness covered with the white face of one of your lowliest creatures.

Bless this funny creation and guide it to lead others to you, to share their tears, loneliness, fears, and hopes. Keep me worthy of this calling, Lord, a holy fool, a minister in disguise.

And, O Lord, as I get older and more tired, give me the energy to keep up with the task, the calling you have set before me: a ministry of love in strange garb.

10

Simply Sitting

A deep cold, propelled by fifty-degree-below zero windchill careening through trees along our river bank, crept rapidly through the house and my wool socks and sweater one February weekend. No fuel oil, no heat.

Three flickers and you're out: sleet, icy wires, wind, no power the following weekend.

Forced by the elements to curtail my usual mad dash through weekends as well as the days in between, I rediscovered something this winter I hadn't realized I'd lost: the art of sitting.

The loss hadn't been sudden, and pain from its extraction not acute in the beginning.

Symptoms began slowly. First came a vague uneasiness I was possibly wasting time, or at the least, not using it efficiently. Life became lists, neatly checked off and filed. Organization and efficiency were the names of the game as I strived to work to my full potential: wash dishes while talking on the phone, leave fires to burn alone, never put off anything.

Discomfort intensified each time sitting was attempted. Pain increased in proportion to whatever important task was left undone. Until finally, in the last stages, sitting was impossible.

I was cured. Now I was a truly productive person. Yet I missed the time I'd previously spent simply sitting. Some of my most splendid, impossible dreams had occurred during those times. I also missed scenarios in which I played heroines, starring in glorious flights of fancy. Gone, too, were times of nostalgia, of replaying certain moments too good to enjoy only once.

Sitting was worth retrieving.

Once its loss was faced and accepted, I relentlessly pursued the missing habit, forgetting, of course, that the more frantic the pursuit, the more impossible the recovery.

In our instant-mashed-potato world, it was difficult to know where to look. Leisure has become big business, and free time is categorized, programmed and marketed. Weary families and individuals are pummeled into pleasure.

Sitting is gone with the wind. It has become suspect, lumped together under the heading "wasting time" and providing idle hands for you-know-whose playground. Children, swinging on garden gates, are told to "find something to do." Families are urged to go, to play, to enjoy.

Worn out from the pursuit, I paused one evening by the fire to reconsider approaches. And, like an elusive butterfly, contentment returned to rest upon my shoulder. I was once again simply sitting.

In celebration, I from that point sat by the crackling fire, on the floor curled in a quilt, at my oak rolltop desk, and bundled up in the snowy woods. Sitting occurs now at midnight after late meetings, by dawn's straggly early light, and after lunch on the porch. I sit with my family, with my shaggy dog, but mostly with myself.

I browse through life with an eye toward possible places to sit. Recliners are good, swings better, and rockers best.

Not only are sitting places comfortable, they are spots for collecting thoughts — not to mention fragmented lives.

Prayer

I think I pray at you, Lord, not to you, on the way to work in the car, between crises and wash loads. There's no time for contemplation, for meditation, for silence.

I want to slow down, sit down, and recapture the stillness from within that restores and renews. Instead, Lord, I substitute a "change of pace," but it's usually more frantic than the daily routine. In my prayer life, my leisure, my creative moments at work, I bombard myself with the ticking of a great productive metronome always set at the fastest notch.

Give me the power to coast, to slow down, to be still and know not only who you are, but who I am to become.

Send me your gift of silence, of stillness, so that I can hear and know.

11

Stains, Spills, Splatters

We had spaghetti for supper last night — almost.

I hollered a final warning downstairs for the family to head for the table, and the dogs flopped expectantly beneath the table in mouth-watering anticipation.

Draining the spaghetti as everyone rounded the corner, I watched the steaming noodles slither out of the pan and into a sink filled with a greasy skillet and sticky bowls.

Silently the family listened to explanations about hot steam, slippery handles, and contrary lids. As one, they turned to the pantry for the peanut butter, grabbing the cereal and milk on the way.

Oh, well, nothing new they agreed. Mom has been, still is, and probably always will be a klutz.

They crunched their way through tomorrow's breakfast and spread liberal amounts of jelly on sandwiches, along with liberal amounts of long-suffering sighs on my ears.

I'm not sure if such an affliction is inherited, and, if so, where I got it. None of our family legends boast of ancestral clumsiness. But perhaps that knowledge has been carefully secreted away in the back of a genealogical closet. I've passed it on to at least one offspring, a graceful gymnast who walks from the tumbling mat where she's flipped and twisted high in the air, only to trip over the painted line on the floor.

We klutzes, though, are not without our endearing charms. Who else provides such lively anecdotes as soon as we're out of earshot? Who else is such a source of "live" entertainment when on the scene?

I've gradually evolved from merely colliding with desks, chairs, bedposts, and table legs to greater feats. And few who know me would be surprised that the sole of my moccasin is emerald green, the color of the ceiling beams in my husband's home office.

The simple act of making a telephone call is catastrophic for klutzes, especially when they are walking the dog. It seemed simple and efficient the day we'd taken a drive into the city. I needed to check in with the office, and the dog, tired of riding in the car, needed to walk. So my husband let us out of the car at an outdoor phone booth. While waiting for an answer on the other end, I patted our new puppy. How, don't ask me, but I entwined the pup's leash through my long, dangling necklace and around the coiled phone cord.

Crouching on the floor of the booth, I whispered my way through the call, my conversation muffled against the dog's fuzzy face, the message punctuated by happy canine kisses. No one stopped to help. Passersby who noticed, guffawed their way on down the sidewalk, where they attracted my husband's attention. He knew, he vows, whom he would find on the other end of their laughter.

So why did he let me paint his den? Simple: he didn't know about it.

Nine years is just long enough to procrastinate before completing the building of a house. This was the year to tie up loose ends, of which his projected den was one. Finishing it began as an anniversary surprise.

I secretly picked out a wonderful paisley wallpaper,

started cleaning out the room, and stirred the paint. Before long, I was so far into the project, the "gift getter" had no choice but to help! Next year, he begs, "just send me a card."

Truly, we agree, though, I outdid myself with decorating ideas, and I worked diligently each night after work and supper. No time to waste, for who else but a reporter who can't function without the looming threat of a deadline would set herself up so dangerously? I'd invited everyone for Easter dinner and the unveiling. A host of family would be the perfect audience for the surprise.

In a hurry to meet my own deadline one hectic midnight, I didn't take my eyes from the paint roller I was wielding overhead to put the final touch on a ceiling beam. About-face at the corner, and I marched my foot smack dab through the paint pan sloshing with two inches of emerald latex.

I match, though; the wild paisley wallpaper from which the green got its day of glory is glued forever tightly to the knees of my jeans. However, on the big day diners noted that my moccasin and the ceiling beams matched the snazzy Easter-basket grass centerpiece.

I have to wonder, though, are we klutzes the only ones who live like this? Are we the only ones to pick up faulty cereal boxes, dribbling sugary crunchies up and down aisles? To spray and starch — not wash — stubborn stains? Are we the only ones who cause cash registers to run out of tape when we walk up? Toll booth receptacles to jam? Copiers to misfeed? Revolving doors to spit us back out the way we started?

We excel in the kitchen, too, and I've carried a trail of blazing dish towels unknowingly over my shoulder till a telltale odor alerts me. Separate an egg? Sure; shells in the batter, yolks on the counter.

I've never been a major casualty to myself, however.

Other than a few broken toes, smashed fingers, and minor scrapes, I've suffered no serious bodily damage at my own hand. Except for the time I broke my ribs.

Nothing dramatic or unusual about the incident: I simply fell *up* the basement stairs. The doctor added insult to my injury as he clutched his own sides, envisioning the scene.

As I reminisce about past exploits, I recall a set of robin-egg blue footprints, size eight, marching crookedly, probably there still, up the sidewalk of a former dwelling, a reminder of a hot summer day, quick-drying paint, and my usual finesse.

Life for most may be just footprints on the sands of time, as poets suggest. But for klutzes, our mark is a bit more indelible.

Prayer

Might as well laugh as cry, Lord. I did it again. I am such a klutz, an embarrassment to myself.

I used to look around first to see if anyone saw me, and then I'd skulk away after picking up, straightening, or fixing whatever I'd done. Now, I invite others to laugh with me. Why not? Sometimes it is funny.

Do you chuckle along with me, Lord, as I pick myself up and plow ahead? Do you shake your head at my antics as my mother used to when I bumbled around?

I know, Lord, that if I'd concentrate on one thing and keep my mind on what I'm doing, I could avoid much of what I stumble over. But there's so much to see, to do, to think about.

Keep me safe from real harm, though. Keep me vigilant behind the wheel, or wielding a butcher or paring knife, scissors, and paper cutter. Help me to pay attention.

Keep me laughing, Lord, when I slip on the banana peels that follow me around.

A good laugh has been a gift from you all these years. Humor, even when we are our own punchlines, is healing. It helps the lungs, heart, mind, and spirit, they're discovering now, and can even be a tonic, a medicine for ailing bodies. But you already knew that, or we wouldn't be blessed with belly laughs even in tense times.

Ready chuckles are better than ready knuckles, and we are usually only too ready to be mad at the check-out clerk, the secretary, the tollgate attendant, even ourselves (especially ourselves?) when we function less than perfectly—such as walking in paint, falling *up* stairs, spilling supper.

On a tough day, Lord, when a laugh might help you, think of me, a special daughter easily spotted by her green moccasin and flaming dishtowel.

12

Tarnished Teakettles

The holiday countdown tolls merrily across wintry days. Procrastinators are warned to get their festive act together and do it soon.

I hear the summons amidst last year's neglected resolutions that return my gaze in frosty windowpanes. Sticky with summer's leftover fingerprints and autumn's crusty insects, they mock my current frenzy.

For during yet another year, perfection succumbed to higher priorities: good books, drowsy summer naps in the wicker swing, chats with friends, puzzles shared with Beth, impromptu basketball games with Rob to show off Mom's special hook shot.

But now company is coming. It's time to unpile closets and camouflage the house with order and spic-and-spanliness.

Someday, though, I'm going to throw a "come as it really is" party. Guests can wear broken-in shoes with the little toes cut out for the pet corn. They can sit in slacks that really fit—not the too-tight ones that beg to be loosened all evening. Refreshments will be common fare, fit for everyone's diet, and served casually on paper plates.

The dilemma of what to do with the laundry will be

solved then, too. Why do I pretend we never get our clothes dirty? Don't my guests also have mounds of grungy jeans, damp towels, and tangled tennis socks in the middle of the floor? Simple math exposes me to the least intellectual guest: five people times three pairs of jeans, six towels and shirts plus two sweatshirts multiplied by three briefly worn sweaters, divided by an average two loads washed daily at bedtime equals a mess.

But, influenced by glossy, perfect-home magazines and a fear of what others think, I spruce up my image. Laundry hides in the washer, dryer, closets, and behind doors. The dog gets dunked, the silverplate polished.

But all that and more will change during my reality party. There may be eggshells in the sink, a ring around the tub. The dog will be as dingy as the sock brazenly left draped over the chair where it landed. The tarnished teakettle will whistle cheerfully from a boiled-over burner, and gooey fingerprints will identify users of the cluttered refrigerator. My Weight Watchers utensils, usually whisked from view, will agree there's more of me scrunched into control-top mythmakers than meets the eye.

And we will talk then, really talk, not chatter, about ourselves, our concerns, and our ideas—not about the guy down the block who lost his job or the couple fighting next door.

I wonder, though, as I contemplate the ashes in the overflowing fireplace, whether folks would come as they really are. Would they enjoy an evening of life as it really is, dirty socks and all? Or do they, like me, alas, try to play life as we think it should be or wish it were, right down to gourmet food, ringless tubs, and clever, brittle conversation? Probably no one would come, being politely busy elsewhere. And do I have the nerve to pen the invitations?

Still, winter's first snow is sifting past the kitchen

window, a moment to share. How peaceful it would be to curl up with an apple and a good book, a pot of chili set simmering for friends to share tonight, candles on the table to hide the dust.

I may reconsider. This could be the year after all.

Prayer

How silly we are, Lord! We dress up like children at play, scrunched into ill-fitting clothes and roles to impress those who are trying to keep up with us.

Help us kick off our shoes, Lord, take down our masks of pretension and perfection and be real. Help us risk being comfortable, ordinary, salt of the earth. Help us reorder our priorities—right neighborhood, car, church, clothes, hobby—to the right response.

We're phony in such silly, laughable ways. But we keep others out and ourselves in through ways that are not funny but sad. How can we be reached when we are untouchable, spraynetted, manicured, lawnmowered, and landscaped into perfection? Is this the abundant life you had in mind?

For just look at us, Lord. How can anyone with a little pain dare track it across our freshly mopped lives? How can anyone with just the tiniest flaw or fear confess it to our carefully created faces with painted-on smiles?

Shake our motives, Lord, jostle us from middle-class snobbery and comfort. Help us throw open our doors to the world waiting just beyond them so that what we have received from you becomes available to others.

Help us see the beauty, the opportunities of our dog-eared lives and homes. Help us to be real, Lord, truly, fully real.

13

A Byte at a Time

"Hi, I'm Bob, the tele-computer, and I'd like to chat with you," a rugged male voice invited when I answered the phone.

Chat with a computer? How? Did he have ready answers for my responses? Am I—are we—that predictable? Where is a Margaret Anne programmed into his circuits?

Curious, I let Bob ramble about his interest in my home: did I own it, was I thinking about selling, what type mortgage did I have? But some things only my banker knows for sure, and he's not telling. Bob would just have to wonder, his information about me incomplete—unless he was going to get it elsewhere, probably from a fellow computer.

Symbols of our present age, everyone seems to have one or more computers. One plugged-in family has nine, with one in the pantry.

Faster learning, higher grades, better jobs: computer literacy promises all that—and heaven, too.

But for every Apple there may be hundreds of worms: spouses "interface" with the Commodore instead of each other; preschoolers sit before blinking screens instead of the sandpile; parents buy infants software instead of soft toys; schools prescribe computers as a technological quick fix for illiteracy of other sorts; students and job seekers squint with narrowed vocational vision, scurrying after the latest promised land; churches index members into orderly files, reducing to a number those who are folded, mutilated, and spindled by life.

And, as columnist Sydney J. Harris remarked, "The real danger is not that computers will begin to think like men, but that men will begin to think like computers."

And so we blunder into a future also resplendent with megatrends and robots, Jedi and genetics, tripping over trick questions such as, When do progress and technology become fancy tools of idolatry?

No matter, too, that I am at heart a high-technology dropout; computers continue to remind me of their importance in my life and how little I matter to them. Unexpectedly hospitalized earlier this year, I quickly lost track of bills and correspondence. Payments were made past due dates, and many folks still wait for my letters.

Friends are more forgiving. Immediately, I received frosty reminders from one company's computer that my payments had not been received on time. On their heels came legalese questions about the state of my memory, for surely I'd merely forgotten. Within two months, I received ominous, but sad, notes regretting that a collection agency was due to receive my delinquent account.

My rage mounted in proportion to the computer's disregard. For I'd included notes with all payments, visited the company's local credit office, and called the 800 number explaining I was not using the account, was making regular payments, and would catch up quickly.

"Hi, I'm Jim calling to apologize for our computer," a charmingly southern voice soothed across telephone wires one day. "This is my job," he explained. "I make calls all day to people our computer ignores. It doesn't know about your surgery—or really care." He chuckled. "So, I'm calling to say *we* do care, hope you're feeling better, and have no problem with your account. Please pay no attention to our computer's notes to you, because it will continue to send them," he said. "It just doesn't understand how people operate."

When Adam tasted that first fruit, he bit off more than he could chew. A parable for today? Perhaps, as we're tempted again by a delectable Apple and other tasty bytes of knowledge.

For computers can figure out all kinds of problems, except the things in the world that just don't add up.

Prayer

We've found another golden calf, Lord: the computer. Truth is written not on tablets of stone but on printouts.

Lifting high the technology that rules our lives, our jobs, even our entertainment, we worship it. Whatever ills befall our lives, schools, and governments, a bigger, smarter machine is surely the answer.

But our offices are becoming inhuman, mechanistic assembly lines. Workers are forgetting how to talk with one another. We can shop, bank, eat, and get answers to our medical questions without seeing another person.

It is not good for man to live alone, we used to agree. But the more of us there are, the more alone we're becoming, the more we substitute things for people.

Help us slow down, Lord, to reconsider our priorities and goals. Keep us on the path to a creative future—a blending of man and machine.

And, too, forgive our arrogance, our pride in our own accomplishments.

Withhold your wrath, Lord, at our latest idolatry. Be patient, for no matter how smart we think we are, we are but children wandering.

14

Training Bras

Everyone is the child of his past.
Edna G. Rostow

Breathing a relieved sigh, I turned the last page of a comprehensive article on stressed-out children, confident that adults are catching on to a need for solutions to protect our children from kiddie burnout. Perhaps I would write a letter to the editors complimenting them on their poignant article.

Short-lived relief: I turned the page. There, spread across two full-color pages, was a team of professionals selling a car. Sleek, red, racy, and obviously fast, the car was being rated by "the experts," the ad copy read. In white coats, no-nonsense spectacles perched on their noses, pencils in pockets, and clipboards ready in hand, the experts exuded knowledge.

The product being peddled was a battery-operated toy "real" car, the experts were children in adult garb.

I wrote the letter all right, but with a suggestion that they put their money where their mouth is. Which, upon reflection, I realized they had done, child consumers, or parents on their behalf, being the market they are.

The hurried children of today. They are molded, rushed, groomed, enriched, tracked, and organized right through and beyond childhood. Prime targets for merchandisers and dream peddlers, they are prey for sellers of everything from training bras and toddler beauty contests to child pornography and childhood stress.

"This little piggy" is not the only one going to market, and baby- and child-store shelves vie for the consumer's attention with image-conscious clout. Designer crib wear (forget plain old sheets) and signature toddler togs (forget stretchy rompers and overalls) squeeze young-sters into the upwardly mobile molds provided by their upwardly mobile parents who are used only to checking the bottom line.

Children are having children themselves. Escalating violent crimes are being committed by children at younger ages each year. Many of today's stressed chil-dren pluck out all their hair, withdraw into clinical depressions, insomnia, violent behavior, ulcers, cardio-vascular ailments, anxiety, suicides, and learning diffi-culties, requiring treatment and medication just to get through their days.

Days of golden youth. Pressures are tarnishing that, however, from parents who push too hard and expect too much too early. Parents pressure not only them-selves to pursue fulfilling, challenging careers as well as provide wonderful houses, vacations, best schools, quality day or after-school care, stimulating and enrich-ing extra-curricular activities; they also pressure their children to excel at these, to "get the most, be the best, go the farthest." And there is pressure not to break under the pressure, which might be a reflection on Mom and Dad that they are not providing something.

That elusive something called childhood, a buffer zone between infancy and adulthood, is being squeezed out of our culture. The twigs that are being bent are not bending, they are breaking under the pressure to keep up, authorities cry and urge us to simply look and listen to the children.

But which way is the modern twig to go? How can we be their parents, grandparents, teachers? By retreating to teach them in isolation safely out of harm's way and running risks they will perhaps grow up stunted and fearful? Or by fighting the system and its demands, insisting that summers of leisure are better bets hedged against a meaningful future than excelling in computer or enrichment camps, summer school, or three sports teams?

Another riddle, another opportunity.

Without consideration and intervention in this runaway lifestyle, our children will have no past—only a wishful, angry longing for what they missed.

Babies have been walking for centuries, but the first step is something that can never be taught. It is a discovery each child makes him- or herself. Why can't we allow our children these and all such experiences without our pushing them to happen?

Prayer

When I was a child, I got to speak as a child, but oh, Lord, today's children have so little childhood and youth. They have to put off childish things before the new is even worn away.

Forgive us our exploitation, our marketing of our children. Admonish us quickly, Lord, before we raise a generation of vacant-eyed, jaded, unimaginative, competitive, and depressed children who have no laughter or leisure, no keepsakes in the treasure chest of memory.

Help us see that we adults are being sold a way of life that builds our own images of success. And forgive our willingness to use our children's triumphs, their apparent adjustments to our fast-track careers, to pin medals on our own chests.

Guide us to be polite to our children, to thank them for the help they give around the house, to appreciate what it costs them for us to be away and to tell them so. Humble us so that we can face them at their eye level, Lord, rather than hurrying them to stretch to ours for conversations about their feelings on empty houses after school, day care, fast food, and hectic schedules that interrupt their dawdling (a most valuable adventure).

Forgive us, and help them forgive us, too, Lord, for we are thieves in the night, snatching away their gift of childhood.

Comfort and strengthen us when we do realize the folly of our ways and begin to change. But trip us up soon, Lord, before we progress ourselves right out of hope. Show and tell us, Lord, that we can't exchange the way of life we've bought into: the no-refund sale of our children.

15

Merry Yule Flu

The family that nosesprays together stays to-gether—for what seems like forever.

In the spirit of the season just past, we gave one another the flu. Believing it more blessed to give than receive, we hoarsely announced, "This is for you."

Each gift was unique, bearing personalized symptoms: coughers received headaches; sniffers got sore throats; stomach upsets were shared with those whose sinuses dripped.

Separate glasses, cups and medicine bottles accumulated on the window sill: his, hers, mine and yours. Those healthy at first barricaded themselves in germ-free isolation, shouting greetings from across the room. They swilled orange juice and popped vitamin C to ward off the inevitable, for soon we were a totaled family, 100-percent stricken.

And we'd had such grand, ambitious plans for a Christmas to remember: pageants, packages, pressure. We'd planned it all, down to the last gift tag and pitch-in dinner, and in yuletide frenzy had added a 500-mile overnighter as the star on our tree.

But as the days progressed and casualties increased, we settled for simply sipping tea together, lulled by

illness-induced lethargy into companionship—a new gift in the toes of our Christmas stockings.

Frantically worrying, listing, shopping, and wrapping, we'd usually shared holiday greetings with notes on the refrigerator or memos pinned to pillows. Our conversations too often had echoed with snippets of impatient retorts, absent-minded responses. Greetings from our family table, alas, were we honest, had resounded with "Bah, humbug!" from the dregs of our holiday cheer.

But the fragrance of this Christmas was mentholated and new. Pine and bayberry mingled with pungent cough drops and antiseptic gargles.

Santa, poor fellow, could've used some help. Gifts bought before the siege were wrapped between coughing spasms. But most of us found gaily wrapped IOUs beneath the tree we'd managed to prop in a corner. Carols were sung with a holiday wheeze, and unsigned Christmas cards lay neglected on my desk. Jobs were missed, school books unopened, and the laundry, like the malady, reached epidemic proportions.

Christmas Day came and went in a feverish blur.

But there are worse things than enforced rest and shared convalescence, even during the holidays. Brief, hectic visits hither and yon were canceled. We didn't spend what we didn't have this year, either, so January won't be bleak with blizzards of charges to leave us stranded. And no one seemed to miss what they didn't get. Too weak to be interested, or even able, we didn't overeat. There was no lingering around heavily laden tables; half-eaten cookies dried beside untouched candy and fruitcake.

And the familiar tale of shepherds and wisemen, birth and promise came alive like never before in the midnight candlelit telling. Its message unhampered by trivia, hope was free to enter our uncluttered lives.

The days of recuperation following Christmas were mild, relaxed, and greatly savored.

Our lessons were learned. We listed new resolutions: more rest and exercise, less hassle, regular mealtimes together, and an apple a day. And soon there was a new comfort to clutch to our still croupy chests, the medical announcement that the flu-stricken multitudes across the country had gained immunity. A nice thought, but we've laid in a supply of chicken soup and aspirin just in case.

Stored away with the twinkling lights and fragile glass ornaments are the blessings in disguise left beneath our tree this year. May they not tarnish under the onslaught of the next twelve months; they'll be the first treasures we unwrap next year.

Happy New Year.

Prayer

Every year I promise to do better the next. I'll start earlier, quit sooner, plan better, shop more wisely. But it took the flu to get my attention to the questions I need to ask: Is angry, busy, frustrated, overworked, and in debt the proper mood in which to welcome your Son?

I didn't think so either, but I was unable . . . okay, I admit it, unwilling . . . to give up trying to do it all. Christmas is the worst time of year for "fixer" types of people like me. We try to make up to everyone—rich and poor, relative and stranger alike—at this one season all the inequities they endure the rest of the year.

Like the lonely relatives I let go their own miserly way the rest of the year; like the poor; like the little kids who only ask to not be smacked around just this one day; like my own family that has had its share of troubles this year. So, overboard, overextended, overwhelmed, I do too much. And by the time the shepherds wander the church aisles in their dads' bathrobes and the angels sing a little breathlessly off key, I don't care. Actually I do care, but about how quickly it can be gotten through, how soon life can get back to normal.

I forget, of course, that after that special day, life need never be normal, that I need not try to do it all, because you have done it for me, for all of us. All we need to do is to stop, listen, and accept the Gift. I've learned this year, Lord, even as I still cough in the night, that I need to redirect my energies and find ways to share your peace and caring instead of my do-gooding frenzy. Maybe a picnic in July with those relatives. Maybe serving as guardian ad litem twelve months a year for those misused children. Maybe sitting bedside-ready with growing-up children when they ask, not putting them off. Maybe walking autumn trails with an overworked husband. Maybe serving meals on wheels for those old people. There are ways, Lord, if I want to bring Christmas to others as it is brought each day to me: a chance for new beginnings.

And from the midst of all this year's confusion, I thank you for this wonderful family. I can say that now, since we're all able to be up and about. There were moments, Lord, that I wondered if Peace on Earth even had a fighting chance with us. But you came, and we were more ready than ever before. Maybe now we'll have enough sense to keep a little of what you gave us this year: a chance to be still and know.

16

Bombs Away!

It was a rerun of a rerun, and the original wasn't really that great.

But, again, I watched the end of the world as I know it. And the end was pretty much how I expected it would happen, how I used to practice for it to happen.

The first time I saw *The Day After,* the television movie about a nuclear holocaust, was on my birthday. The best that can be said for this week's rerun is that I've had five chocolate cakes blazing with birthday wishes since the movie's first grim forecast I might not have many birthdays left.

But "What goes around, comes around," a snippet of current thought observes, and I approach middle-age birthdays under the same threat as when I arrived, squalling, in the world.

Born just a few weeks prior to Pearl Harbor, I nursed upon fear and uncertainty from parents and a world surprised by attack. A toddler, I crooned a favorite ballad, "I love a sailor, and he loves me, too . . . coat of Navy blue . . ." to an uncle returning from the war. Aftershocks from that war's star, The First Bomb, shushed my song to a whisper even though

I didn't understand why the grownups put fingers to their lips.

I climbed trees, roller-skated, rode a bike, and studied atomic blasts as a youngster in Knoxville, Tennessee, the third-most strategic city in the nation at that time due to our proximity to Oak Ridge Atomic Laboratories.

A bit of drama still clings in memory from those days. Recently digging through a box of old family keepsakes, I found a "show and tell" I'd proudly displayed in grade school then. My favorite, it was a radiation measuring badge issued to my father to wear when delivering printing from the family business to a nearby war industry.

Just think, I bragged to classmates taking turns to touch the small metal treasure on a sturdy chain, my family would be the first on the block to accurately measure our level of radiation in the feared war which, at that time, seemed terrible but survivable.

In those grade school days, instead of fire drills shrieking sirens alerted us to "duck and cover" drills, and we hid from fallout crouched beneath wooden desks. Sometimes, herded by anxious room mothers on hand to help, we "evacuated" into cars leaving town.

Determined not to be separated from my family during the "real thing," however, I prepared an escape route from school through alleys and back streets to our house where my mother and baby brother waited. I planned during anxious nights how to get my father home, too. And how I could take my dog.

Radiation badges got lost, unthreaded from their chains that carried roller-skate keys; evacuation routes got interrupted by new highways. We're not going to practice war no more, I lullabied my babies.

Years later, though, came a new battle, not the war for which we'd practiced, but the first one fought in the living room. After the dishes were dried, the diapers folded, we counted the bodies carried across our television screens. Bodies of kids killed while we car pooled our own not much younger; while we mashed the potatoes, grilled ribs and chickens, and tossed a salad.

In the midst of this "traditional" battle, our nuclear consciousness was raised, our anxiety increased by Cuba, missiles, and deterrence, and on the silver screen as we and *Dr. Strangelove* walked *On the Beach*.

Like old home movies, rewound and shown over again, those early childhood nuclear nightmares have returned for many of us. For me, this time, though, they are brought into a different focus as I am a wife and a mother.

I doubt that I worry alone, and I wonder where are my classmates from the late forties and early fifties who studied war in the gym-turned-theater. Where are the others of us who sat through color movies of atomic bomb tests, staring in marvelous dread at the mushroom clouds bursting like fireworks over the playground of our childhood? Where are those childhood resolutions to avoid disaster? Were they thrown away with the earnest lists we had to diligently copy of what rations to stockpile in shelters, along with the calculations of how far and fast the concentric circles of radiation could travel that we had to memorize like times tables of doom? Who else recalls the guilt, the fear, from playing the simulation games of "Fallout Shelter" in the sixties, where decisions about who got in and who didn't were left pounding on the door of our consciences?

When does experience become wisdom? When do rehearsals become so dreadfully realistic that the actual performance is canceled? I can only echo T. S. Eliot's sad epitaph, "We had the experience, but missed the meaning."

The search for peace of mind, if not peace, through

building up weapons is not new, and history suggests that weapons built are weapons used. So far, wars have been "winnable"; so far, though, even debate on this next one isn't.

So I watched *The Day After* again amidst much less furor than the first showing. See, it didn't happen, some say now, pooh-poohing worriers who were again urging viewers to take seats in the front row. It could happen yet, they warn.

Scrambling about in this "peace gap," many of us are caught between the crossfire of doves and hawks, lefts and rights. We are torn between those who look forward to a nuclear holocaust as a rapturous second coming and those who foresee it as our own fiery apocalyptic failure.

Squabblers on both fronts, though, keep missing the target, the question being detonated in our living rooms on prime time: "How can we prevent this?" Bumper-sticker slogans are weapons as useless as despair and apathy; all options toward hope must be considered.

I know a great place for us to meet and do this. It's on the east corner nearest my old elementary school, right under a wild plum tree where an evacuation arrow used to be nailed. Imagine it there; take a long look at it, and then let's all join hands and head down the direction it's pointing toward safety.

Anyone know where that might be?

Prayer

Fire next time. I recall that promise someone made. Or was it a prediction, Lord?

I might feel better about fire, not flood, Lord, had I not seen those first proud clips of film shown to impress the impressionable school children, had I not learned those enthusiastic lessons about how vital it was we learn to count the seconds between stages, to do the math that would equal our safety if we could move fast enough.

No one can count, or run, that fast, we now know, Lord, but still we keep playing with fire like disobedient children. Afraid of getting caught, some take their country's nuclear tinder and sneak away and ignite their blazes underground; others offer theirs, from blueprints to bombs, to the highest—and angriest bidder. Still others trundle wheelbarrow loadfuls home to hoard like bones in the lawn, "just in case."

In case, Lord, just in case.

I might feel better about fire, not flood, too, Lord, if I didn't ply my trade on a computer like the war referees do also—that electronic vital link between the "just in case" bluff, call it deterrent if you want, and that fire coming next time. If we can't cure the common cold, how can we hope to cure computer viruses, the newest plague to worry about, one which could start an epidemic of war through the tiniest glitch?

At work the other day, I lost the same story three times, Lord, gobbled byte by byte by a capricious, sophisticated, and usually reliable computer. A squirrel lost his balance and fell into a power line—something that rarely happens, but crash! there went my story. Reset, the computer system crashed again, and again.

Don't they have squirrels between Here and There, Lord, along power lines strung through the countries who've chosen up sides for war? Lines that are already clogged with fear, suspicion, and hair-trigger philosophies instead of communication?

If it's fire next time, Lord, I doubt that it will be your hand igniting the tinderbox that is our world; it will be ours.

So, tame us, Lord; march us onward as if to peace, not to war.

But just for a minute, please listen to me, Lord, just me, in the midst of this cosmic concern, for I am worried for me and mine. Spare me my dreams, those motionless gaps of time where I feel as if I'm swimming in molasses, my feet are going so slowly. Like a craving for chocolate, I've had these dreams since childhood. Then, I couldn't reach my parents, my dog, before the evacuation car pool took me away; now I can't reach my husband, my children. Two dogs, now, and a cat, Lord. My family. Please keep them safe.

Help us all to see that "my" family must come to mean bigger than five people, two dogs, one cat, and six pots of red geraniums, Lord. That "my" family must mean the world, and that this family must gather around one table.

Either that, or even you won't be able to extinguish the fire with the tears you'll surely shed over all your children who insisted on playing with matches against your wishes.

Shalom, Lord?

17

Long Friendship

I was a "show and tell" last week. Actually, it was more like a "show and point" by the time J. A., my three-year-old friend, and I arrived at preschool where he'd invited me to visit.

There, confronted by classmates and teacher, he buried his head in his mom's knees, mumbled and pointed toward me, suddenly overwhelmed by the mouthful, "This is my friend Margaret Anne from Indiana."

I was warmed by his inclusion of me, his mother's old friend.

Love—and friendship—is a mirror, a two-way looking glass that reflects our best selves. And even our not-so-best selves look good as their reflections return to us spit-shined by the delight others express in just having us around.

I'll defer to wiser heads than mine to decide who most enjoyed my Christmas gift, an airline ticket to visit my long-time friend six hundred miles east. Was it I, the receiver, who was able to flee daily routine and winter blahs? Was it the friend and her family I was "given" to? Was it my husband, the giver, who stayed home alone in peace and quiet?

Surely all of us.

For long-time friendship is the richest of all treasures, spilling over like foam on a brew to flow across all that are in its path.

We met in the turbulent sixties, she a youth group member, I a leader a mere five years older. Then, we blended our voices in "We Shall Overcome," a theme song of the times and later of our friendship that's buffeted by distance, professions, ages, life stages, and styles. In the nearly two dozen years since we met, we've added husbands, careers, moves, and children, often going months without conversation or communication, so that each reunion is a surprise.

And now, like tufts of fur and snips of twine, her nest is feathered with Brownie meetings, practices, piano lessons, and misplaced boots and mittens from young children.

Emptying of childhood reminders, my nest, however, is brimming with drivers' licenses, college campuses, and maps to get to the nests of my fledgling children who are building their own.

So my friend and I pause, needing to linger briefly in the other's kitchen—caretakers of very different flocks, but as connected as the seasons that both take us farther apart and draw us closer. For no one can understand the ebb and flow of life, especially of being wife and mother, as well as one who rides the same wave at just a slightly different spot and is willing to share the view. Fore- and hindsight are gifts of long-time friendship, a sturdy craft.

Thus, my faint melancholy at no one needing me now to button, zip, boot, and comb became celebration last week as I did it again for her three children, my fingers stumbling and stiff from disuse.

We scurried to their van going this place and that, as young families do, and I marveled that I had ever daily done this at all. And had enjoyed it. And now enjoyed not doing it.

Perhaps my friend will enjoy it more now for seeing that. Her weary wonderings, echoes of mine not so many years ago, are posed by all mothers, especially those of us with other careers: "Can I find the energy?" "Will I last as long as this stage?" "Who am I?" Wonderings that can fade in the face of new stages like my freedom, a vision she is drawn to like moth to flame.

Too, when we're together I see where I've been, she where she's going, as we swap experiences in the barter of friendship that sends us both home satisfied.

Our children, friends also, bound by nothing yet linked by history, watch from different spots on the playground of childhood. Mine, the "big kids," and first to leave home, revisited that childhood last week on the wings of the butterflies carefully drawn by the "little kids" and sent home with me to tape on our bare refrigerator.

Too quickly my four days passed, marching double time as they do on all vacations. I had planned for that, though. Sometimes obnoxious, I know, with my ever-present camera for preserving special moments, I had taken new film and fresh batteries, intending to devote a whole roll to our visit. But we were too busy making the moments to pause and snap many pictures, and I came home with space left at the end of my roll.

Like our friendship, it waits for the next exposure, winding forward always with room for another day.

Prayer

What a wonderful surprise, Lord! And you know how hard it is to surprise me, snoop that I am. I never had any idea a new husband and an old friend were conspiring. I'd barely dared hope that a new husband and an old friend could even be politely tolerant of one another. What a gift is friendship, old and new.

And those children, what a delight they are to watch growing up, from my vantage point as a borrowed aunt. The oldest, born on my birthday, gets as much delight from that coincidence as I do. The youngest, born the same week my mother died, rings a circle of eternity around me each time I see him. The middle, the first to befriend my new husband when he first was, shared her gentleness. Their jokes and their banter carried us on chuckles into a new friendship.

Perseverance is not a trait much in demand in this instant-mashed-potato world where everything is created to be obsolete by the time you get it home. Yet this special friendship, born around a church group campfire, is like the ancient cars we drive: sturdy crafts to get you where you want to go. Each dent, each scratch and nick has a history that grows richer with each telling of the tale; each year of our friendship does, too. That was a close call, that time when we hesitated, toyed with trading it all in, backed up and started again. The only reason we pulled it off, Lord, was that old-fashioned gift of perseverance you instilled in both of us.

They are too far away from the airplane now for me to pick them out of the crowd, Lord, as I head home. But they are there, the youngest waving his arms like a plane, engine noises revving (I can imagine the van ride home). I am glad I am going by real plane.

Thank you for being the God of surprises. And I was, Lord, caught off guard and surprised, too, that when you promised to be making all things new, you even meant old friendships.

18

Century of Life

Sometimes I can see no farther than the end of my nose. Like barbed wire fences, circumstances form a tight boundary around my view of future possibilities, and I sit, stuck.

Work is exasperating today. My kitchen is cluttered, the library is empty of books to entice me, and the yogurt shop is out of peanut butter flavor. To top it all off, I can think of no excuse to cancel today's visit with a ninety-six-year-old friend.

But duty calls, and I suck on the lemon-drop piety of my martyrdom as I drive through a thunderstorm to the nursing home. My shrunken world is framed between the windshield wipers: life through a dirty fish-bowl.

And what does my friend have for me? A copy of her just-published fifth book, a small collection of thoughts, ideas, a view of life as seen *Through an Open Door.*

A sucker for any book, I thumb through it, asking her a little loudly, for her hearing is a bit off today, why the title.

To invite a closer acquaintance with her world many don't want to see, she explains. So she's provided a view into this carefully orchestrated hustle and bustle of swishing, white-stockinged legs, a rattle of pills in a cup, a squeak of tires on polished tile floors.

Through her open door—regulation heavy duty, fire safe, and wide enough for wheel chairs and emergency carts—she notes it all, sharing her view with any who take the time to look behind the softer-voiced, slower-gaited residents of the community that is a nursing home.

If there were ever a narrow expanse of life, this must be it, I muse from the arrogance of one who has escape from it in the parking lot.

A resident here for nearly a decade, she speaks first-hand of misgivings and worries, of loneliness and fear. She also speaks of contentment, security, and relief, challenging stereotypes as well as the blackest moods; and mine fades as I skim a chapter, a remembrance.

She was a first face when we moved to town, a ragtag family of mismatched adults and adolescents, those self-conscious offspring who feel they fit nowhere, especially in a new town.

"Come to my home," she invited our oldest, an uprooted lady-child at the braces-and-bashful stage.

She joined other young people each week at this new friend's apartment—already compressed from a spacious home on a tree-lined avenue—where they discussed essays they'd written the week before and listened to her music, she to theirs; where they played games and shared ideas and great books; where the quivering lumps of teenage self-doubt were refined and expanded under the care of this vintage woman.

Many of them, adults now, were the hosts of her autograph parties for her other self-published, sold-out books.

When her capricious heart pulled one too many close calls, she was first to point out the need for a move to safety, a move to a home which has added to her life rather than subtracted. It is a home where her writing desk and favorite rocking chair gather around a table of books and a dish of candy, which I pick through for the minty ones, a home where I rock the afternoon away behind lace-curtain rain.

A home in which to write.

For, of her five books, three have been written here. And only, she admits with a mischievous smile on her dried apple-doll face, when someone hides pen and paper, will she be done.

As she works, she anticipates—looks forward to— moving someday soon into Another Room. The view into it is made less frightening by looking at it head on, she confides, for even it is full of promise.

I sang of that promise for her last Sunday. Having had nearly a decade to practice, I got it pretty well right.

I've both dreaded and looked forward to singing for her since that afternoon she first asked me to share my music at her memorial service.

"Die? Surely you're not planning to die," I spluttered, aghast.

She took my hand, this friend who's fought life-threatening diseases longer than I am old, and told me the selections to practice.

She wasn't there to hear me and nod her head in rhythm from her favorite pew or rocking chair. Surely, though, that was she humming with me in the stained-glass shadows.

There are few things to do when a friend dies, so I was relieved to have my songs, not a casserole or cake, to take to commemorate her passing. As friends do, she's blazed a path for me, a novice at aging, at going on beyond each milestone, even grungy-windshield moods.

The theme of her memorial, of course, was "Maybe I can," a litany many have repeated after her so long we're doing the special things she never questioned that we could. So it was only fitting that I bid her farewell with a thank you sent over the divide that separates us in a song she requested.

Dear friend, I hope you enjoyed it. It was my pleasure.

Prayer

Dear Lord, keep me treadling as fast and as long as I can in my favorite rocking chair. I crave speed, the wind in my face, new ideas, and places to go that draw me forward.

But when I can't move, when my quota of energy is an outing a week, a spell in my rocker only once a day, then, Lord, reconnect my body's energy to my mind and to my attitudes so they'll always be looking outward where possibilities are as close as the door or window.

Thank you for this dear friend who taught me to weep and then walk on, to dream and do, to be always moving in order to be there to meet you halfway when the journey is done. To a reunion, she said, like two friends.

Yet, I don't do this willingly. I would pop today's vigor and happy, youthful mood into the deep freeze, never to change. Feet planted, chin stuck out and hands on hips, I defy old age to just try and take me.

O Lord, when I think about aging, the things I have yet to do clutter my vision like the snowflakes flicking themselves like spitballs against my windows today. Help me to see that aging, like being born, like living, happens one day at a time. Slow my fears and anxieties; quiet my angers.

Grant me the sense to mourn youth only as a butterfly cocoon that must crumble to let the new creature free. Give me the healing gift of tears to mark each passing stage from last birthing, last wedding, first grandchild, last grandchild, last revolution of my own body's cycles of replenishment, first lonely night of widowhood, even last day in my own home.

Give me at the same time open arms to receive and nourish what is planted and growing on the fertile fields of possibilities where these tears fall. Give me joy in the harvest, a harvest time, Lord, where you and I can barely keep up with me as I shuffle corridors in whatever home, here or there, when the time comes. Let's keep busy, Lord, till the very end.

Thank you for the gift of aging. May my greedy youth, feisty forties, and reluctant middle age ahead not stand too long between what possibilities this stage, too, can offer.

Pacemaker, walker, cane, and replaced body parts, Lord, I'm prepared to try them all with your steadying hand under my elbow.

19

View from the Summit

Forty years old this week, and the view from the summit is breathtaking as I venture on "over the hill."

Much leaves me breathless, though, since the only thing I consistently jog these days is my memory.

But life is supposed to begin with this birthday, and I'm ready. Accumulating my gray hairs springing into prominence has been no small task. I carry hoards of wisdom around my middle like saddlebags of truth.

Kids, jobs, an eternity of lost sleep, about 25,940 meals prepared, and hundreds of car-pool miles have crisscrossed smile and worry lines, blending them into character across my wrinkling brow.

And, too, older is "in" these days, as Sophia, Shirley, and Liz tell all about the marvelous middle years. Far from hiding truthful birth dates, today's older women sparkle outspokenly. From pages of popular slick magazines, they share secrets of how to be better, not older.

We mellowing middlers, a recently discovered pot of consumer gold, are maturing right on cue. Coached from the sidelines by squads of Madison Avenue cheerleaders, we enter the magical middle kingdom of keeping fit. Appearing eternally young, we are charmingly wise and wrinkle free.

Ladies' jeans bend and stretch with the aging figure, no longer quite as flexible despite being lavishly anointed with rejuvenating creams, fortified by oat bran or fiber, and prodded by tonics and alphabets of vitamins. Our hands are dishwashed into youthfulness. The lucky ones are often mistaken for younger daughters.

Yet I'm astonishingly content. I'm no longer intimidated by computers, permanent press continues to delight me, and I've outlived the new math. And, thank goodness, the game may not yet be over; someone whistled at me the other day when I was walking back to the office from lunch. That's good news for someone to whom whistling usually means the teakettle is ready.

Scanning this year's birthday almanac, I find I'm in good company with those whose lives were enriched after forty. Erma Bombeck, patron saint of humor, began a new career after thirty-seven, becoming a syndicated columnist after forty. At one hundred years of age, Grandma Moses was still painting, a talent she didn't develop until later life. James Michener began writing after the fortieth mark. At eighty-nine, Albert Schweitzer was director of an African hospital. And who could overlook the ageless charm of George Burns, who at eighty years of age received an Academy Award for his performance in *The Sunshine Boys*.

The only ingredient missing from this week's birthday potpourri is the wisdom I once attributed to those at my present age, wisdom still elusive and yet to be attained.

But perhaps that will come with age—whatever that is.

Prayer

I've been so young so very long, Lord. It's a relief to reach a milestone birthday. Young in school, young in the office, young in my faith.

Perhaps with age has come an awareness of your

presence, your restraining me, saying it doesn't have to all be done now. I've learned to hear you, Lord, through the years together. When I was young, all I could hear was my quick response, my certain answer. Always me, I, my. But now I know that alone, no matter the age on my driver's license, I'm still very young. Instead of my hearing going, it's coming!

And, too, Lord, how can another birthday pass without saying a thank you for not only the years, the opportunities that have been mine, but for those who've made my life a real celebration throughout every year, not just in November.

Spare me, Lord, and hold up a mirror should I begin to dislike my gray hair, my laugh and wrinkle lines. Let me see that to grow, to age is beautiful. Remind me that to stay young, permapressed, massaged, and starved into perpetual youth is to worship my own reflection. It is to ignore the person you see, that you are still creating.

Help me age gracefully, full of laughter and ease. Help me respond to your gift of yet another birthday with curiosity about where we're to go next.

May there be many more, Lord. Happy returns of my day.

20

Toying with Gifts

I don't know . . . Christmas gifts appear to be hazardous these days. Several swipes up and back toy aisles, a.k.a. the "Fright Zone," this month leave me disappointed, dismayed, and disbelieving.

'Tis the season to be jolted, not jolly.

It's the selection I need to check twice, not my list, for it's filled with special people.

At the top of it is a five-year-old friend. I wanted a special gift for this most special friend whose name I wrote beneath the jaded title with which I'd christened my list, "Merry Christmas, anyway."

"Blaaaaaat!" creepy, disfigured rubber balls with vile breath say to me when first I walk past them. Their bloodshot eyes stare across the aisle at the kids whose creators surely must dwell at the bottom of the garbage pail of taste and sensitivity. Center of controversy, they've been elevated to the status of collectors' items by young and old alike.

Dolls cavort, slink, slurp, burp, fill diapers, talk back, whine, kill, capture, and torture. Known and chosen by brand name, they, too, appear more status symbol to own than cuddly offspring to love.

The smarter ones cover their ears to shut out the

incessant barking of stuffed, mechanical dogs whose frantic yap, yap, yapping urges someone, anyone, to please take them home. Battery-powered symbols of substitute love, these mechanical mutts aren't best friends: no childhood secret would be safe with these stiff, sad creatures who obviously tell all they know.

It isn't difficult to walk past packaged "theme" toys where a single toy boasts everything (ask any child for the inventory) from sleeping bags to beauty set, wardrobe to video, book to underwear, cartoon to movie—the better to lure you, dear shopper.

From overexposure in recent years, I've developed a slight immunity to this merry mayhem of holiday gifts. Oh, I know, some experts assure us that violence, grossness, and frenzy don't harm children. Fine. Time will tell. I think, however, they might harm me! I can't imagine myself as a grandma stuffing stockings with rude bad-breath balls. Or a bomb. Or a doll whose love is programmed into a few one-liners.

Between now and the grandmothering days, I vow with a last look around, the four thousand new toy selections developed and peddled each year and I will arm wrestle one of us to the floor.

I leave the toy store, moving on quickly through the mall to ties, bedroom slippers, earrings, and gadgets for the rest of the folks on my list.

By the time I wander to the ice cream shop to console my cynical self with a double dip of comfort, I've accepted that I am going to be a disappointment, if not outright failure, to my young friend come December 25. Thanks to her, I've found out this year who's naughty and who's nice. And I refuse to buy from them, not wanting to leave even the proverbial lump of coal in their coffers.

Back to the top of my "anyway" list. No lasting problem even if I can't find a toy, I think, brightening. For, in keeping with my usual tradition of buying others what I want for myself, I decide to get her a book. Draining the last ice cream through the tip of its cone, I start for a favorite bookstore.

Hold on a minute! I stop midstream, to the consternation of shoppers running into me, and quickly step to one side of the busy traffic flow. Stirring like a nibbling mouse in my birdseed bin, a small thought has been tugging all day at my fly-away coattails.

Isn't the Spirit of Christmas the point of all this? it asks curiously. Aren't hope and promise of better things to come the biggest, brightest, most beribboned presents beneath any tree?

Well, yes, I mutter grudgingly. Not quite ready to give up my frustrations, cynicism, and concerns, I can't, however, ignore this optimistic little mouse-thought.

I never make it to the bookstore, for I am side-tracked into a candle shop. I buy twin holly-berry red tapers, plaid napkins, and two pewter napkin rings engraved with love, a keepsake message of the season.

A holiday tea party is set and ready; a fire welcoming us both into my festive keeping room as sanctuary from the wintry chill and relentless yuletide shopping blitz.

My dogs, dirty and noisy, but loyally real, watch at the window, their tails wagging in delight at my friend's arrival. Abigail the Wonder Cat cleans her white fur collar and mittens, primping in readiness from her spot on the mantel.

Sugar-cookie dough waits in the refrigerator for our young and not-so-young hands to cut into stars, stars that lead past cynicism, frustration, and loud, unruly and contrived gaiety, stars that lead toward a Silent Night that passes by us ever so softly each year whether we see it or not.

Watch, listen for it. In the meantime, Merry Christmas, anyway.

Prayer

What a cynic I am this year, Lord. I'm such a sad sack I can hardly bear to be around my own sad and surly self. A real holiday treat, that's me.

But things are topsy-turvy. The holidays are getting "fouled" up, if you catch my meaning. Those bad-breath balls are really gross; the handicapped cards are hauntingly awful. What are they teaching our children?

I must confess, Lord, that too often lately I've been teaching them how to complain, criticize, and despair. It really doesn't matter that reality validates my attitudes, which have a bad breath of their own. I know, because I caught a glimpse of myself in a store window. If I'd been a child seeing me, I would've run the other way. Fast. I looked as fierce, gruesome with my scowl, as some of those toys.

My rage at the toymakers and vendors has twisted me into a parody of a holiday shopper. Maybe I should send the toy designers this as an idea for a doll next year: Granny Grump, Holiday Shopper. Look, boys and girls, see how she scowls when you push her a little too hard. See the slingshot she carries in her knitting bag to twang you with if you offend her.

Oh, Lord, thank you for that picture. I feel better for laughing, even at myself—so serious, so righteous.

So correct, too, but being so overwrought is not the solution. And being so angry and ready for violence, even if it is only with an imaginary toy slingshot, explains a lot doesn't it, Lord? For we are an angry, frustrated, spoiled, and greedy little bunch. It always seems worse this time of year, when who we could be contrasts so sharply with who we are.

Please, dear Lord, as my Christmas gift this year, bring me something to soften my attitudes, to loosen my features from their worried scowl, to lighten my outlook. Shine, like my cookie star's light, your creative power into even the darkest corners of our commercialization of your son's birth.

Help me, too, most of all, not to get stuck, like last year's worn-out toys, on the shelf of despair and cynicism.

Guide me into finding creative gifts that will help you and me bring to those on my list what I most want for them: a sense of wonder and joy when they open their eyes Christmas morning onto your gift of Presence.

Merry Christmas, Lord, from Granny Grump.

21

Nightmares in the Closet

Beth will sleep soundly tonight, but I won't, even though lights are burning brightly.

Visions race through imagination of axes embedded in foreheads, children fleeing bloodied pursuers, women taped, tied and trapped beneath grinning assaulters, houses that tilt and turn: media monsters served with popcorn and pizza.

Zippered into her new sleeping bag at last night's slumber party, this youngest daughter encountered horrors on late, late movies and brought them home with her.

We'd told her not to go see the movies when they were at theaters, and she hadn't. But, with the logic only a child can master, she put the dilemma to us today when she came home: how, in a roomful of other girls, could she not watch the movies that were on the television in front of them all? She, she explained, couldn't sleep through them, nor could she get up and leave the room. Why, we never quite got straight, except I suspected a big dose of peer pressure blocking her exit.

So, she was a "captive audience." Her first belligerent, defensive defiance when she dragged through the door today at "having to watch" the forbidden movie, however, began turning to uneasiness after supper.

Tree branches became clawed hands, fingers reaching for plump, ripe souls and bodies; fall winds chasing dry leaves down the sidewalk were limping monster footsteps inches behind you. She spent most of the evening looking over her shoulder and turning on lights.

What effects do horror, violent sex, occult, and gross entertainment have on young, impressionable minds?

Not to worry, assure some, including the parents who approved the fright movies for the slumber party. Children need to know what's real. And they need to get rid of fear and aggression and anger, they explain, citing such movies as surrogates for action.

Worry, others insist. Copycat killings, mirror rapes, and imitation murders are being linked to movies and television.

The demons bred in Hollywood and delivered on prime time and video rentals have become members of the family. Welcome? Or outcast?

Locked in familiar battles with evil, parents must outwit the demons' creators, and the parental apathy that nurtures them, if the tide of violence is to be stemmed. Yet, beware lest the concerned become witch hunters, book burners, or pious puritans who see evil everywhere.

Balanced solutions are hard, but not impossible, to come by. A simple no might work for some but not all children. More difficult to schedule but necessary are creative alternative activities, watching movies and shows together, discussing reasonably with children why there are concerns over certain sights and sounds. Essential also are helping them believe in their own ability to overcome the fears and bad aftertastes they get when they do see or hear something awful, and helping them develop skills for not getting "stuck" in fantasy, hooked on the highs of violence. Unraveling the commercial tangle of nightmares for profit, perhaps we can turn out the night lights. Hopefully, we can tame the megabucks monsters waiting to frighten our children and us.

Finally ready to face the night, daughter leapt the wide chasm between the rug and bed, flinging herself beneath the covers. Head under her pillow, she buried her fears and blotted out the terrors lurking beneath the dust ruffle on her bed. Sleeping with the light on, to the annoyance of her cat curled beside her, she exorcised the demons in a fitful rest.

I, down the hall, worried less about her than about the unstable minds who soak up this stimulation as gospel and goal. A child molester I once interviewed kept an orderly collection of pornography filed for ready use. A young boy who used to play in our yard, abused by a violent father, fashioned his wardrobe, vocabulary, and quest for power on an avenging movie superhero who blasted his way in and out of trouble. The only difference was that the actor and the police he battled used blanks in their guns; the boy, grown into a troubled teen, and local officers, didn't. Their shootout had no happy ending. Beheaded cats, disturbed graves and churches, death curses, and coded messages caused the police and community to wonder where some young people had gotten their frightening ideas a couple of seasons ago.

Connections? Surely.

For isn't popular entertainment both a reflection and a stimulant of society, leading to an undercurrent of violence wherever you look? Hasn't the acquisitive eighties, with its selfish, self-righteous disregard for colleagues, the poor, and the weak, spawned a growing underclass, primed and ready to retaliate? And, on whatever screen they look, they can see how it's done. A circle of violence, with fiction becoming fact becoming fantasy.

For some, violent entertainment is simply that; for

others, it is a blueprint, it is empowerment and even permission to get what they want or to get even.

All I want is a good night's sleep, without the light needing to be left on to ward off the dangers, real and imaginary.

Prayer

I had to leave the light on all night for Beth, Lord. But no locks were strong enough, no bulbs bright enough to keep out her fears. There are no assurances convincing enough to cast out the demons.

And my imagination ran wild, too, as "bogeymen" invaded my dozing with horrific possibilities.

Reality is bad enough, Lord, without having entertainment fearful, too. But how do we fight big business and those who don't care? How do we withstand teasing and challenging about "overprotection" and "smother-mothering?" How, too, equally important, can we remain separate from those censors who practice equal violence against our young by withholding all but the most narrow views of life? We need to find a delicate balance between the two extremes.

Yet I yearn to protect our young. They can never unsee what flickers across the silver screen. Numb, or overstimulated, they turn to us for assurance against what we paid to let them see. Aren't they perhaps also frightened by our lack of setting safe boundaries for them? Yet if I protect them on the one hand, I thrust them onto the firing line of their peers, those "everybodies" who do it, on the other hand.

Give me courage, Lord, to blunt my edges to the pressures and provide better alternatives. And when that fails, keep me ready to listen, to discuss the latest horror, the most recent evil deeds.

Be with us during the senseless darkness of our leisure.

22

Sandwich People

Slapped like pastrami on rye, many women these days are finding themselves sandwiched between conflicting loyalties: aging parents and their own families.

Like the two friends who invited me to grab a quick lunch with them. "It had to be between exercises and piano lessons," the one who called to make the date apologizes today as our lunch is served. "It's Mother's exercises, really her physical therapy, but we soften the description, and the girls' piano," she explains, cutting into a tomato with savage swipes of a knife.

I am the only one who notices her vehement slicing. Our third for this hasty lunch is too busy scooping soup into her mouth, crackers in her pocket. "For later," she explains in response to my raised eyebrows. "I'll eat them in the car on my way home, because I have to be back before one o'clock. The sitter leaves then." I am momentarily confused. Her children are teenagers, long past the need of sitters.

Pondering this, I miss the beginning of her story.

"'Help me, please! There's a man in the closet,' she cried," pointing a shaking finger at the shadows stalking her from between clean blouses and dresses. "Their

110

hangers were bones rattling, she told us," my friend relates.

And then I understand. The sitter is for her mother, who's come to live with her after Alzheimer's sidetracked a fairly independent old age.

She is telling us of a child's nightmare. Such things are usually soon soothed by the gentle but firm reassurance of a parental voice. But now the soothing voice is a daughter's, the nightmare's terror her mother's.

Is turnabout fair play? we ponder over a second hasty iced tea refill. Less than fifteen minutes before departure time, they warn me, explaining, "Good sitters are hard to find, and you don't dare be late."

I nod as if I understand, although I don't, not really.

The turnabout-fair-play question is a hard call, for the quickest answer is certainly.

Who has not wondered what a parent is owed? Who has not dreaded being asked to pay the debt, real or imagined? For it can come due in the ringing of a telephone. "The hip is broken. I can't stay alone any longer," shatters routine, privacy, and independence as completely as the bones.

Trouble is, there is no operation, no stainless steel pin, that can set straight this sudden intrusion, we agree as we synchronize our watches. I've gotten caught up in their clock monitoring.

There are going to be more daughters, daughters-in-law, and even granddaughters tapping the faces of their watches to check the ticking away of their free time: people over sixty-five are projected to outnumber teenagers two to one by the year 2020.

Multiply the two friends sitting beside me by that number, and there will be a lot of iced tea drunk while figuring out the answers. Guilt unites today's two daughters hastily gulping theirs as if it were a prohibition libation. Guilt is the biggest burden, these two confess, crumbling crackers into communion wafers, the

111

iced tea a drink of new life as I pass the pitcher around again.

"It's awful, but I really don't want to be bothered with taking care of someone else. I'm so selfish," one begins, the other finishing her confession, "It's like taking care of an eighty-year-old toddler, and I want to go camping this weekend," she spits, her ferocity embarrassing us.

Involuntarily I glance at her skewered tomato.

Guilt begets anger, and how can a "good" daughter be angry at a parent who nursed, nurtured, and nudged her offspring into adulthood? How can a "good" daughter turn her back on tables reversed when she is the one being asked to clip toenails, shampoo hair, button blouses, change wet beds, fetch meals, brush teeth, tie shoes, cradle and hug?

In essence, it's being asked for a return to early childhood, except that childhood is a time when a parent does it all as investment in the future. But this time, there is no hope that the "child" will grow up, gain independence and move on, relieving parental burden. This time, someone else must help relieve this topsy-turvy distribution of parental burden acted out by the children stumbling about as if in the "dress-up" clothes of another generation.

A pamphlet I brought, just in case this came up, is shared. It's a colorful brochure about a support group for this sandwich generation. I give the group my whole-hearted approval and grab for the lunch bill.

My treat, I explain, not adding that a dozen dollars is a small price to pay for my freedom waiting only a parking lot away. These struggles are behind me, and I would not call my parents back from their rest to endure this stage again for all the delight I'd have in their presence.

No siree.

Permission to feel this blessed relief from the companions guilt and anger can also be found around a

112

perking coffee pot, center of this support group I once visited, I tell these friends as we hurry, hurry to the parking lot. The agenda was brief, coffee hot, and routine brisk, as women in all stages of parenting their parents listened and talked. And understood, I stress to my friends, who truly believe no one else does understand what they are going through.

This group, and dozens of others like it across the country, have a simple secret to success: the old formula of supply and demand. More elderly needing care equals more daughters needing support for giving care. "I am not alone" is a common denominator for these women who ask one another the unaskable questions: Is it wrong to feel abandoned when I myself need a mother to lean on? Will I ever be able to sleep through the night again? How will I feel if Dad dies in the nursing home he didn't want me to put him in? Can my marriage last through this? Am I doing enough? too much? too little?

"Answers?" my friends prod me. "Will we find answers?"

"What good are answers anyway?" I respond. "It's the asking that is scaring you, so go and find out," I urge, shooing them on their way as we guiltily realize we've overstayed the clock's allotted segments.

Like these lives that have become complicated by others' aging, its golden hands have swept into another hour.

Prayer

Honoring our parents has come to mean something really complicated these days, Lord, and I think we need some help figuring out just what you meant by that.

Did you, even in your infinite wisdom, ever dream that someone could die and yet take years to be buried?

Doubt me, Lord? Well, let's just stroll beside some

beds where sheets cover little more than a few brittle bones kept together with flesh as thin as airmail paper and a sleek, whishing pair of electric lungs. Lunch is served through a shunt tucked like a napkin under the chin, a high tea in droplets freefalling into the right arm. Dinner? I don't know, Lord, nor does the diner, having been unconscious for three years.

Tell us what to explain to our children when Grandmother dresses and redresses herself hour after hour after hour. Fill our mouths with explanations that satisfy when we tell Mother she must return to the nursing home this afternoon; she'd only been out for a visit. What do we tell Father when he's brought home after driving for hours in his pajamas and a baseball hat, without a license? Give us a script for how to tell him we're taking away his keys.

Oh, Lord, what anguish it is to step into shoes we'll never fill—our parents', those wonderful, strong people who've always been larger than life to us but who now don't even recognize us as their children.

Comfort our uneasy knowledge that we're just glimpsing who we, too, will be one day: the aged ones.

Send us the wisdom to know when enough human intervention is enough, when the mechanical pulse has beaten long enough, and courage to act on it, especially if it's the patient's will to say when. Be ready with your mercy when we err, which we are certain to do as we learn how to handle such power, Lord, between life and death. Blessing and curse, Lord, are these high-tech possibilities in which we live and will die.

But for now, gently lead us, your daughters, Lord, as we learn new mothering skills for how to take care of our parents, today's task. I know we can do it, for you have instilled in us kind hearts, gentle but firm hands, and soft laps.

And, O Lord, we challenge you to help us see how our maternal gentleness can exist with our rage, sadness, and rebellion at having to do this at all. We'd thought we were finished with dirty diapers, food in the hair, naughty children who run away from us in the store. Modern medicine and our own determination to thwart death as long as possible have brought us to a strange sight: a playpenful of aging parents.

Bless them, Lord, and empower us to be able to lift them lovingly into our arms.

They're a heavy load.

23

Time Turns the Page

Skipping down the sidewalk . . . silky brown braids bouncing in rhythm . . . glancing backward, just briefly . . . sitting with a friend on the big yellow school bus . . . a snaggle-toothed grin framed in the window . . . saying good-bye to Mom and the dog sitting, waiting on the porch . . . the first day of school.

Reading, writing, 'rithmetic, meeting them all . . . reaching the highest rungs on the jungle gym . . . report cards, ballet, scales on the piano . . . cooking backyard stew in the shade of a tree . . . falling, breaking a leg . . . giggling hints of secret first loves . . . adopting the forlorn and collecting strays . . . protesting injustices encountered too soon.

Long-legged and lanky, singing down the yellow brick road, star of the grade-school play . . . swaying from the top branches of a favorite maple tree . . . games of pretend, forming a club . . . learning to skate . . . bouncing for miles on a red pogo stick.

Playing games in summer's twilight . . . catching fireflies in childhood's dusk and wondering where they flew when released from a gentle, grubby grasp . . . riding a pony, sweaty in the sun . . . discovering barn kittens, nestled in a dusty oat bin . . . dressing for tea parties and ginger cookies, cutting rhubarb for a pie . . . two-wheeling, freewheeling on a bright blue bike, hair flying behind.

Cheerleader, athlete, songbird, and poet . . . growing fragile and intricate, yet surprisingly strong . . . hair too short, or too straight, or too curly and long . . . counting freckles with dismay . . . braces and bosoms, curlers and mirrors . . . taking a stand and stamping a foot . . . tackling new issues . . . sometimes fighting alone.

Raising a hand in a gymnast's salute . . . leaping, vaulting, victorious—high in the air . . . filling the gym with silent joy . . . long dresses swaying, never missing a step . . . waltzing through memories on a warm May night.

First kisses, dreams, learning to drive . . . phone calls, finding a job . . . shared secrets, concerns, traveling alone . . . skirting the nest's edges, leaving childhood behind.

Hurrying down the sidewalk . . . long brown hair feathered by the breeze . . . tassle swaying in rhythm . . . gown tucked under an arm, diploma the other . . . marking a passage . . . glancing backward, just briefly . . . spinning the tires up the hill . . . a fleeting, thoughtful smile . . . saying good-bye to Mom and the dog sitting, waiting on the porch . . . the last day of school.

Prayer

What more can I say, Lord, than I've said to you since even before she was born? Watch over her, guard her steps, and visit her with your presence.

She was a gift, Lord, I know, and it's time to let her go. But I can think of so many other things we've not done. I remembered a question I never got around to answering, a story I was too busy to hear. Forgive me, Lord, for perhaps not being all I could've been while she was my little girl. But thank you for the gift of this lady-child.

Does her laugh delight you as it does me? Does her singing soar to wherever you are? We've done a pretty good job, Lord. And I know I couldn't have made it this far without your guidance and strength.

But be with me now. It'll just be you and me, I fear, as she leaves the familiar and ventures away. And I find I'm far better at roots than wings. Free me, Lord, from grasping the apron strings—loosen my hold. Help me to trust—both her and you—that nothing can separate us from your love and that this is only the beginning of another era, a possibility.

Help me grow up, Lord, as the children do, too. Help me be there for them as you are for me. Go with her today. I mustn't follow too closely, and I can't judge my distance yet.

24

Sampler

Mustard and russet. The tweed yarn I'd draped around my neck for a second opinion in the store mirror was a perfect match with my new down jacket. I bought an extra skein for fringe and mailed the package of yarn for Mother to fashion into a scarf.

Her knitting needles clickety-clacked back and forth day and night, she happily reported, and my scarf was growing. Maybe enough yarn, she hoped, to make mittens. Thumbs only, I reminded her.

Vests, scarves, hats, baby blankets, a wooly lamb for a grandson, an afghan—drawers and closets testified to Mother's love. Her "to do" list was steadily increasing as were her self-taught knitting skills.

"Come down," the unexpected summons interrupted my busy life. "Your mother's in the hospital."

Had she taken my yarn with her to hospital, I wondered while buying my bus ticket. The car's worn brakes wouldn't make it up and over the mountains, and Saturday was no day for getting them fixed.

As soon as it could the next day, the bus left the interstate for its one-track business and wandered onto the narrow asphalt trails carved in the hills. We wound for half a day past dozing hounds, tender young tobacco plants sprouting in the pale misty dawn, swinging bridges lashed across rock-strewn ravines, skinny-dipping youngsters in a farm pond.

A Sunday morning, other people were traveling, too. Carrying noon pitch-in dinner fixings in baskets draped like purses over their arms, women got on, then off a few miles later to attend church first.

His Bible, a best friend held closely by one hand, Preacher, as the regulars hailed him, used the other hand to hoist himself aboard the bus perched at the top of a mountain. A quietly smiling elderly gentleman polished to fine ebony, he sat second seat from the front. In spite of the humid southern heat, he was bundled into a wool overcoat and felt hat as if still chilled from the racist winters it had taken him to fight his way up there.

We all joined him in urging the driver to hurry. "Don't want to be late," he agreed, turning eyes the color of a good-luck buckeye toward me.

I was, though.

Cancer, like the kudzu vines strangling hillsides and roadways we passed, was creeping through Mother's body.

I looked first for the yarn, my scarf, when I reached the hospital, unable to quell my frantic search. There was nothing familiar in that antiseptic room, a place of dangling tubes and vague mumblings from doctors who fled a dying patient, young in her sixty-fourth year. No place for yarn, it was instead a waiting place where life was for certain only under a nurse's stethoscope. A mocking place, where collard greens and hush puppies clattered on plastic trays. Happy, nostalgic meals, although untouched, their aroma drew her a chair to the childhood table she visited in morphine dreams. "Momma? Is that you?" she smiled, waving, to a spot on the wall above my head as I munched a hush puppy.

It was early, even as days are measured in a hospital,

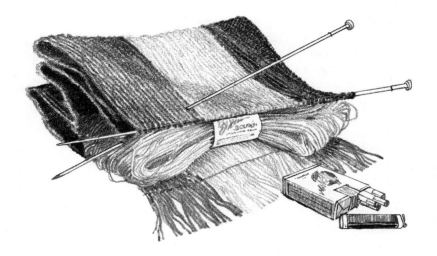

when I first arrived, and I thought to vigorously join up sides in a tug-of-war with death. But the score was settled by shadowy X rays, and we quickly switched sides not to prolong her painful losing battle.

No sense in returning north. I was there for the duration, becoming one of the regular lobby loiterers clutching our telephone quarters. Those ahead of me hunched over their messages, their backs turned to the glass doors as they hugged private miseries. While I waited my turn to send bad news home, I made angry lists of those I'd rather see die.

The hospice unit where we moved her was a better waiting place. Its lounge was a sanctuary where several of us were sharing the loss of a common denominator: our mothers. For no matter our diversity, we all have one. Whether tall, short, fat, thin, sick or well, in all shapes and sizes, temperaments and abilities, they are our mothers.

Sometimes to honor them is to accompany them

through the valley of the shadow of death, and to let them go at this threshold where we'd gathered now. All that was left, then, was to kneel beside their lives, their courage, their love.

Still extending it, Mother held my hand—but not knitting needles, piano keys, or cast iron skillets for cornbread—and they seemed surprised at their own stillness.

Yes, she was a knitter, a pianist who accompanied me to rousing strains of "Old Mill Stream" and "Shanty Town" and an attentive wife, grandmother, sister, aunt, and friend. And a smoker.

It was that last that redefined all the others.

Cancer of the mouth had invaded her life, which we'd gathered to guard nearly a year earlier during a seven-hour surgery. We'd hoped it had redeemed the damage done by the alluring weed.

But it hadn't. And as I held her wasted body, I thought, "You have come a long way," just not quite as promised, baby. Now it was her lungs and liver, then it had been in her mouth, prizes for the intruder that had eluded CT scans, tests, and our pleas for her to stop smoking.

Failures at that, we now stood beside her bed, failures at this, too. But then she made a request. Red gelatin. She wanted some red gelatin.

It saved us all.

The nurses rushed to order it; the kitchen to stir it up; the dietician herself to deliver it; and we, her family, to spoon two meager swallows into the hungry mouth.

Later, I watched, fascinated, as the red gelatin melted on her tray in the sunlight. A blood-red puddle, it was life energy and fuel she no longer wanted. Instead she turned toward her new companion, constant pain. Like a friend, it was leading her from us to relief, its unbearable flames making the bridge to a final healing easier for her to cross.

Tugging gently, I slipped more of her life away as I removed the delicate turquoise-and-silver rings from her fingers and threaded them on a safety pin. A lump in my billfold, they were another bridge crossed.

I prayed for a reversible umbilical cord so I could transfer life from me to her. A repayment, Lord, I pleaded, as I sat sewing on a distraction I'd brought along for the waiting hours, an embroidered birth sampler for a new niece.

Its threads kept tangling, and exasperated I gave it up for a moment's nap. Mother was in a coma, the nurses explained, and wouldn't know I was gone with the rest of the family, but I felt the need to stay for once alone with her.

Exhausted, I dozed in the late afternoon sunlight Mother had so loved, curling around its cushion of brightness when it touched her bed.

Camera-shutter quick, a scene opened for me, and I caught a slivered glimpse of a pond, a hilly meadow, a tree—green, growing and brimming with sunlight. Cat-like, I soaked up its comforting warmth in my dream.

"It's so hard to let go," Mother said, and I leaped from my chair, embroidery scattering as I woke and hurried to her bed. There had been no response, no words for two days.

"Do you want to?" I asked, holding her hand with its marks left by her wedding rings. Measures of life, they wound like circles on the tree in the meadow I'd just glimpsed.

"Yes," she whispered. I promised, and she accepted, my offer to be a companion for whatever length of time she had left on her journey. Toward a meadow? I asked. She squeezed my hand, and we whispered briefly of mothers and daughters, of good-bye.

Are farewells ever said?

But, so soon exhausted, she returned to her coma and I to my chair, but not to finish the sampler.

Suddenly frantic, I took extra care to make tiny stitches, elaborate pains to keep them even. I dared not complete the needlework, I decided, terrified at the revelation that life hangs by such a slender thread.

For on this valley of the shadow of death, there was no imprinted pattern or color key to show what to do next as there was on my sampler, and the needle faltered through my tears.

As if to be part of this, her friends came by, bringing their variegated lives, like snippets of yarn, to share one last time with Mother, and I listened as I embroidered. Memories, prayers, tears, cards, and nosegays of remembrance wove together into a final looping stitch and last taut knot after supper. Removing the completed sampler from its rigid frame, I put it in my purse with Mother's glasses and watch.

That night, the family sat on the floor of her room. Slicing apples and quartering bananas, we split a gift fruit basket and devoured Mother's stash of crackers and juices the kitchen insisted upon sending; communion in hospital-issue paper cups. Tales were told, and I learned Child-Mother had once chased a goat off the front porch with a broom, a story I'd never heard. Hymns were sung; verses recited.

"Hurry," the summons came at daybreak, and those of us sleeping rushed to her bedside.

With a flicker as delicate as a bird's wing, her pulse stilled while we sang our last verse of "Whispering Hope."

Her hospital belongings, not even enough to fill my sampler's rhyming "three bags full" were trundled to the car, her body to the earth.

Later, while cleaning her house, I found my yarn wrapped in the half-finished scarf anchored by her ivory needles. Tossing it over my shoulder, I wore it short and unfringed, as I do still each fall, while I worked.

I pitched the remaining yarn into a garbage sack with her ever-present cigarettes and tarnished lighter. Beautiful unfinished skeins of love unravel and tangle in my thoughts without the slightest warning.

Prayer

I don't belong to anyone now, Lord. I have no roots or anchor. My Mother died today.

Who will recall the stories of my birth, my first steps? Who will tell me I'm perfect and pretty and always welcome me, no matter what?

My mother is gone, and I helped her make this final journey.

Was I right to help her let go? Should I have urged her to fight, to endure?

Yet we all felt your presence close, right there, beckoning. And it would have been for me, only me, to keep her so I would not have to be alone any sooner.

So, I sent her to you on the notes of a hymn, the whispers of our prayers, as she lay in my arms.

Please welcome her as she welcomed me for more than forty years. Enfold her in your arms as she did me in hers. Wipe away her tears as she caressed mine away with her last efforts. Assure her that she is loved and forgiven as she loved and forgave.

I need your comfort, too, Lord.

Reach out to me, a little child again, lost and frightened and all of a sudden alone. Today, I'm no more than a marionette, Lord, and I stand holding my own strings, no one on the other end. Stay with me until I fall asleep and be here should I wake, frightened.

Let me be a child tonight, Lord. Tomorrow I'll be strong and efficient. But for now, find me, hold me.

25

Thorny Nest

Head on my knee, Nutmeg met my gaze, her soulful eyes asking, "Where is she?" Casey, the middle-aged Westie, and I exchanged knowing glances. We knew: our people have left us before.

This was Nutmeg's first stint at farewells to kids going away to college; my third and last. Easier? Hardly.

Not to say that postcurfew pacing, paycheck juggling, laundry washing, meal cooking, and loud-music listening have been easy, either. They haven't.

But neither is cleaning an already cleaned, quiet house, talking to myself about fall fashion and new movies, nor watching an offspring shrinking in my rearview mirror as the car pulls away from a college curb.

I've never found any windshield wipers for blurry eyes, no matter how many homeward bound trips I make. Over the years, though, I've found that a quick stop, a breather, before beginning the long journey back home alone, helps.

An ice cream stand is conveniently located about a good sniffle away from the college home of the two older kids; a hamburger spot is about the right distance from this last child, light years away in another state.

Tears and all, I, wouldn't have it any other way. And I celebrate the timely migration of fledglings raised to fly even as I wonder if I'm not better at roots than wings, those two best gifts we should bequeath our children.

Mother Nature, always nearby, understands. Sympathetically she points the way for those of us who might yearn to lean a bit too far from the nest grasping a disappearing shirttail—a temptation even on the tallest mountains. There, eagle parents share the tasks of building nests. Together, they weave a frame of thorny vines and brambles, twining and bending them into a wreath. This they lace with thistles and prickly teasel pods whose spines grasp the cushion of soft grasses, milkweed silks, and leaves they add next. Here they gently lay their fragile eggs and raise their eaglets.

Then comes the day that Mother Eagle loads the babies onto her wings and soars with them into the highest currents, there to flap them off. She always takes them high enough so that, should the eaglets falter or tire in their attempts to fly, she has ample time to swoop beneath them and catch them on her wings. Once they master flying, they accompany her for a while, then venture off on their own during daily forays for food, always returning to the home nest.

Returning, that is, until Mother Eagle completes her next task in the season's turning: gradually tugging the soft grasses and silky threads from the nest, leaving behind a bare framework of thistles and thorns, an uncomfortable place for tender eaglets to sit for very long.

Seemingly as soon, flying lessons are nearly completed here as well, and those of us left behind survey the empty nests we've worked so diligently to create and see them now filled with success, a paradox of emptiness. It is a success, we discover, that often feels more than a little like sitting on the point of a thistle to us as well. Quick as the upbeat of a wing, though, we parents begin to recall a place we'd wanted to see; a

127

book to savor; a spot of quiet to find; a fledgling's own nest to visit; a conversation to finish.

My season of nest sitting is over, and outside, our basketball is already flat; cobwebs and rust keep score on the goal. The bathrooms are at last clean and dry for longer than an hour; no damp towels mildew on the counter; no clothes wrestle on the floor.

Unable to avoid visiting the most recently vacated bedroom any longer, Nutmeg and I slowly wandered in. Remarkably, unrecognizably neat and bare, the walls and floor returned our blank stares; the quilt squared its corners on a surprisingly made bed. Silence from the absent stereo blared through the late summer air filled with dust motes of remembered songs.

Removing a clean shirt from the nearly empty closet, Nutmeg at my heels, I walked across the room. Nodding to the pup watching me with head cocked to one side, I dropped the shirt in the middle of the floor, a tuft of comfort for brief, seasonal returns.

Empty nests need a little soft comfort left behind, beckoning, reassuring: You're never far from home.

Prayer

What if she doesn't want to come home, Lord? What if she really is gone, leaving me behind? What if—and I can hardly whisper the words even to you—what if she leaves behind all we've taught and shown her, with the dolls on her closet shelf?

I'd not worried about her until today, Lord, when we were moving her into the dormitory. Fried hair; really, Lord, the girl next door to her has fried, orange hair. Short skirts, tight skirts, tattered and torn jeans, and the loud songs volleying across the campus through open windows I was prepared for; I'm a two-time veteran, don't forget. It was the fried hair that reminded me that this is even a new generation from an older sister and brother, also veterans of college life. New generation, new temptations, and new values that mock mine, and maybe this special daughter's, too.

All I could imagine is our lovely daughter coming home for Thanksgiving with her blond curls the color of a centerpiece pumpkin.

When did I become such a doubter, such a worrier? Was it writing news stories about the teenagers who never made it home, detouring into one-way ditches, empty booze bottles flying with them through shattered windshields? Was it photographing teenagers stopped forever in the turn lane, their bodies pinned like moths in the light of revolving ambulance lights too late on the scene? Was it bylining stories of teenagers who, as my grandmother used to say, had seen no need to keep their fun above the belt, becoming premature parents?

Help me to separate the issues, the children about whom I care. Help me to not penalize this lovely young adventurer for errors made by her peers, her friends. Help me always to be on the other end of the telephone line when she calls; always on the porch to welcome her home—a place where she can bring whatever temptation she faces to measure it next to the shape of her family, where we will welcome her, no matter if at first we don't recognize her under a mop of fried orange hair.

Be with her, Lord, as she strolls the college avenues of choice and temptation beyond description, those that promise quicker, easier and less painful ways of growing up than just day by day. Be with her in a loneliness that is bound to creep in when she resists. Help her to see that in the boxes of cookies, puzzle books, and woolly sox I mail along with are wrapped my love and belief in her, are stashed a mirror of who you and I see her to be, a mirror that she can take out and use when her self-image is interrupted or distorted by others' views.

26

Bitter Candy

"Oh, Mother Dear, may I go for a swim?"
"Why, yes, my Darling Daughter:
Just hang your clothes on a hickory limb
And don't go near the water!"
                                    —Anonymous

This little rhyme, culled from childhood memories, skipped into my mind a couple of weeks ago. It was on the day which I later captioned the "Raked Leaves Caper."

I was out walking along our country roads when I spotted new neighborhood children raking and dumping fall's crisp leaves into piles perfect for jumping into. Rake, pile, leap. I stopped to chat with them, only to have both of them hightail it to the house where only a twitching curtain assured me I'd not imagined them.

They were afraid of me, I realized with amazement, as I picked up my pace and completed the first half of my walk. On the return trip past the leaf piles, I was relieved to notice that the mother was out with the children. They took refuge behind her as I stopped, determinedly cheery and, I hoped, appearing as harmless as I really am, to welcome them to the neighborhood. As shy and flighty as the doe that sometimes wanders into our

130

yard, she provided paltry protection to her offspring cowering behind her in the leaves. A beautiful day in a pleasant neighborhood; pity they weren't enjoying it.

With one hand we parents offer youngsters the richest, most stimulating, creative childhood in history; the other hand we hold up as a stop sign: "Warning: life is dangerous."

In worried voices we point out what can, and does, happen to unwary children. For the 1990s child the alphabet begins with *A* for AIDS, and a milk-carton gallery of lost peers serves as a picture book.

"Who's that? What happened to her? Will I get lost, too?" I listened to two young children bombard their mother with questions over dinner table conversation while I was visiting. The troubling centerpiece was one of the milk cartons printed with a picture of a lost child.

"Was it a mean man who took her?" the four-year-old persisted, his eyes wide with concern. I was glad I wasn't pressed for the answers his mother searched for.

When is warning prophecy? What ensures that everything is locked up securely enough to guarantee a child's safety? When do warnings and cautions stunt growth and strand children on the riverbanks of carefree youth like the child in the nursery rhyme—poised and ready but unable to venture beyond? How is it possible to protect without panicking children into neuroses?

Quit worrying so much yourself, advised experts I eventually interviewed, having decided to turn this concern into an article.

Easier said than done, I fretted, recalling yet another conversation with young worriers. Halloween treats started this one. Sadly aware of the way things are these days and wanting to prevent any parental concern about the safety of candy dropped in their children's sacks when they trick-or-treated, I planned to give stickers.

"But what if they have drugs on them?" the visiting child worried, going on to explain that they'd been told at school not to take stickers from strangers, for certain stickers had been painted with drugs, which would "hook you," he warned.

His—and by this time, my—anxiety decreased after I reached a decision to drop half dollars in trick-or-treat sacks. A bargain no matter what it cost me, I decided tiredly after he and his family went home. "Lock your door," was his final greeting.

Fear is good. Appropriate fear, that is. Those of us who have felt excessive fear (and who hasn't from time to time) have also known its paralysis, the feeling of helplessness it leaves.

But little kids have little fears, at least little to our eyes that see the "biggies." Children's fears are bordered like samplers on the nursery wall with that most important word: *my*. Will *my* pet die? Will *my* house blow away? Will *my* friends be nice today? Kids also can't tell the difference between reality and fantasy, often jumping to erroneous conclusions about darkness, dreams, monsters, and death.

Adults, however, fear it all, and usually with the best intentions project fear onto their children who, little rascals that they are, are the family antennae picking up some special event, good or bad. Constant adult and parental warnings tell children that they can't control their lives and are incompetent, an invitation for children to become dependent and helpless.

Instead, parents should inform and teach awareness and safety information at appropriate ages, always communicating a belief in the child's ability to respond with less fear, for instance this season, about witches. And above all, they should convey that they will be ready to listen to the child's concerns.

The mom of the milk-carton incident decided to quit "dithering in my own vague worries" and enrolled in a parenting class where she learned to build her children's belief in their own intuition. Kids' minds hate a vacuum, and as soon as she and her daughter talked about believing and acting on her occasional sense that "something isn't quite right about this," the child quit biting her nails.

The next time my young fearful friends came to stay with me while their parents were gone, I casually steered conversation to a look back to my own childhood and learning how to ride the city bus alone. It took on an adventurous tinge as I confessed how afraid I'd been and that my fear hadn't lasted. That and suggesting we not watch television were about all I could think of to do, and I was frustrated and sad for youngsters who need to learn coping, not avoiding, skills to deal with the very real dangers they face.

An 1812 French primer for sponge divers, *How to Swim with Sharks,* begins with the assumption that it is possible, even necessary, to safely swim with sharks. Information includes learning to counter aggression, control bleeding, disorganize an attack, and assume the presence of sharks. But the message is to go ahead with the necessary activity of diving for sponges. My neighbors play "The Stranger Game" to help their three children develop coping skills to be used in potentially dangerous situations. And to open up conversations, for children need to know that nothing is off limits for conversation with parents and their other special adults who will be ready to listen if they have a concern.

While we wait for their questions, we have to decide whether we want to teach them caution or teach them fear. And before we teach them anything, we will have to decide whether *we* are fearful or merely cautious.

Balancing fear and caution along a fine line is imperative; otherwise, it's "Everybody out of the water," and parents and children alike will become mere spectators instead of active, enthusiastic participants in the swim of life.

Prayer

We're raising a generation of 'fraidy cats, Lord. But it's because we're such 'fraidy cats ourselves. And you certainly know why as well as I do: rapes, kidnappings, spree killings, wildings, molestings, and muggings. Your world has gone mad—our world, really, Lord, for we are the ones who've turned playgrounds, family dinner tables, and marriage beds into battlefields.

Our children can't tell what's real and what's fantasy, often our lack of guidance blurring it for them. We park them in front of television and movie screens either unaware of or uncaring what they absorb. Forgive our lazy indulgences of children who beg and whine to watch and hear what we know they shouldn't. Forgive our failure to establish safe boundaries for our children. No wonder they don't feel safe; we let in all the monsters imaginable!

And at the same time, we must confess, we don't face our own fears, Lord, doing little except wring our hands.

Help us equip ourselves with precautionary measures so that we may lead our children through the valleys they indeed face on any given day. Help us trust our intuitions, be wary, careful, prepared, vigilant, and "street smart." But oh, Lord, prevent us from becoming sour, worrying, fearful hermits who can only watch from behind curtains the world you intended for our enjoyment.

Help us organize and galvanize ourselves and our neighbors into crime prevention groups, helpers, and interveners. Challenge us to be creative in our preparation and protection of our children, so that they don't shrink from living abundantly in spite of the dangers real and imagined.

And, Lord, as we put extra chains on our doors, strengthen our spirits, our sense of humor, our optimism that fear doesn't have the last word in the bedtime stories we tell our children.

27

Get Mad—and Even

"Don't listen at keyholes. You might hear something about yourself you'll wish you hadn't," cautioned my grandmother in memory's ear, delivering yet another homily I had dismissed as a child along with advice to brush daily, tip lightly, swear not at all, and chew slowly.

I should've listened.

On the very day I endured yet another root canal at the dentist, I overheard just how much a certain person hates me. I'd known I wasn't one of her favorite people, but hate? I hadn't suspected, and to think I could've remained blissfully ignorant had I not listened around the edges of another conversation that didn't belong to me.

The worst part of all is that I slunk away, leaving the party early, before I could hear whether the person she was talking to also hates me. Probably does, for enlisting more haters is this woman's calling.

I floss diligently, brush daily if a little tardily, and have given up chewing gum, hard candy, and opening stubborn packages with my teeth. That should prevent some troubles, but I have no idea what to do to stop the decay of relationships.

Should I quit my job? I want to holler at her, since I know that I represent (how I loathe being a category) working women. Working mothers, excuse me, which is much worse. And she maintains that we are at the root of the demise of the family.

Should I go places frigidly alone, leaving a delight-ful spouse to fend for himself, since I know that our marriage-friendship annoys more than inspires her?

Should I quit singing, since I know she says my voice is too loud, too high and shrill, too showy? Should I not laugh, joke, and generally cut up like an errant kid in the back row of the choir, since I know she thinks me immature?

Should I wear sackcloth and ashes or last decade's sensible, predictable garb, since I know she thinks me equal parts flippant and frivolous in my casual fashion?

Should I publish a disclaimer in the newspaper's classified ad, relinquishing any connection to my chil-dren who, about 75 percent of the time, make me proud, since I know hers embarrass and frustrate her? Name a fault, and I have it. At least according to her.

Like a teenager at the mirror, all I can see is this one blemish on my slate of relationships. And, like that ado-lescent, I can't let it alone. I have to pick at it, trying to analyze and evaluate its potential to cause me trouble. But, why worry? I try to laugh it off. I'm a bit beyond worrying about getting asked to the prom!

But injustice rankles, pestering me like a lash trapped beneath an eyelid.

Ever play the old game of "Telephone?" Or maybe it was called "Gossip" in your neighborhood. Either way, try a version the next time a lull occurs in group con-versation. How quickly, how powerfully, bad news travels, which is what has me biting my nails; how fast a poll can she take to find allies against me based mostly on silly, petty, nearly imperceptible annoyances?

At least as soon as the gossips lay their lips to them, blowing them out of proportion like gaseous balloons to float above me.

So, I ask that pimpled reflection returning my perplexity in the mirror, who gets to decide what I get to do? Who I am? Lonely job that it is, I guess I do. We all do, although sometimes it is without applause from those who, for their own reasons, would want us strung like puppets dancing, dangling, under public opinion.

Oh, sure, once I realized we were oil and water, I tried talking with her, only to be ignored and sent away in shame for trying. I see her face in a painting I once admired in a gallery: a crowd of open-mouthed people clamoring, but without any ears. She must have none either, for she quotes me incorrectly whenever I speak.

I used to run into this woman frequently at the grocery store before I found out just how deep is her hatred, how bad she wishes life were for me, and I would exchange pleasantries, tissue paper shallow, but pleasantries nonetheless.

Lately, though, I've avoided the grocery store and evaded her if I saw her coming, uncertain what to do.

If she knew what I sometimes do in choir, she'd add this to my list of faults: I daydream, and yesterday I re-created the shoot-out scene in the movie *High Noon*, where the two enemies walk the dusty trail to blow the other one away. Which trigger finger is the fastest? is the question to answer before the orchestra finishes its dirge.

My grandmother gave me an answer for this duel, too, and I'm already lying in ambush with it behind the cereals if I see this gal coming. Leaping out into the aisles, I'll taunt, "Sticks and stones may break my bones, but names can never hurt me."

Just maybe, a good laugh over the differences spilt between us in the past would be as good a way as any to move on. Knowing how itchy both our trigger fingers are, chances are any duel would be a draw anyway; both blown away, dust to dust.

Prayer

She hates me? Well, then I'll just hate her back, Lord. Eye for an eye, tooth for a tooth, just like you said yourself. Revenge is yours, though, you are reminding me? Well, let me help.

Oh, don't worry, Lord, I'll get my revenge in socially, innocently acceptable ways: a dropped innuendo here, a raised eyebrow there, perhaps a leak or two of information I've gathered about her husband's practices, which, by the way, are no better than they have to be. No one will ever know I'm behind it, starting the ball rolling. Really, Lord, be fair. She started it; I'm just finishing it.

I thumbed the gilt-edged pages of my new Bible searching for the smite-the-enemy passages, Lord. A little Old Testament wrath, a little battle and skirmish, armed with my righteous indignation, felt good. Yet, I don't know how to interleave those passages with the ones that suggest blessing those who curse you and turning other cheeks.

Help me to put the two poles together, meeting somewhere in the middle with a balance of accountability and compassion; a blend of understanding with expectations for better behavior from her; a composite of peace and justice.

For, while it's not okay for her to say hateful, lying things about me, it is not okay for me to retaliate—or to say that it's okay she lie about me. Help me to bring both truths together with the help of your truth: Love one another as I have first loved you.

But, really, Lord, how can you, much less I, love someone so unlovable as she is? I have never prayed a prayer without an end, but this one must be: There is no end to the list of people who hate. There is no end to those who will as quickly hate back.

Turn the sweet taste of revenge in my mouth to bitterest bile, like an unripe persimmon, lest I become drunk with my grudge-holding power, a savory brew.

Help me trust in the redeeming, clarifying process in which fat and facts rise to the surface and her lies will be exposed, and that I'll be left intact in her wake.

Be with me, Lord, as I work through this. Keep me from easy answers that will only mock your promises of true peace. But keep me, too, from holding out too long if a truce can be negotiated. Be at the bargaining table with us, Lord, as we squabble our petty differences, but don't let us linger there long; there are really important matters to see to. Forgive us our smallness.

28

Nothing to Wear

Mother Nature would be throwing her annual spring fling in a few weeks, and I had no idea what to wear.

As I approached my semiannual fashion identity crisis, a hasty survey of store racks crowded with spring frocks hinted that my choices lay somewhere between "quaint" and "curious."

The little-girl look, visibly popular again this year and straight from the pages of *Little Women*, I discarded at once. I never fit the role of demure or frilly when I was a little girl. Hair ribbons were worn drooping over one eye, and my hems were uneven in the fanciest dresses. The pockets of my childhood were not for hankies, but for marbles, bubble gum, and roller-skate keys.

Another possibility, desert wear crossed with a kind of cowpoke, western look, is back in the fashion saddle this year. Bandanas that cost as much as an acre of long-ago land lead the accessory stampede. Chunky jewelry jingled like spurs in my flank as I smoothed down some canvas jodhpurs that didn't need a horse to give me bowlegs.

With an eye to winter's padding on my waistline, I draped myself in tent dresses worn over T-shirts and cinched at the waist with a fringed scarf or two. Instead of fashionable, I merely looked lazy in them, rumpled and matronly. Nightgownish, I told the clerk. Everywhere I looked, shelves boasted signatures of the world's beautiful people who've diversified long enough to urge us to become one of them with a splash of cologne, a tilt of an eyeglass frame, a tweak of the briefest briefs.

Even sweatsuits, the backbone of Saturday armchair athletes, have been touched with the designer craze. Stripes, slogans, logos, and quixotic color combinations are splayed across these once simple, baggy outfits. Alas, they are fit only for Olympic contenders.

After weary hours of shopping, I concluded that in the great flower garden of spring fashion I'm only a weed, and I headed for the car. At my exit, bundling into my muffler and hood, I checked out the pink and white rabbits hopping down a department store bunny trail strewn with scantily clad mannequins. They peeked from behind plastic dogwood while snows still howled across parking lots.

We are simply not capable of enjoying the season we're in. We must frolic in the future.

Or the past.

Which is where my youngest thinks I live along with dinosaurs and other parents who won't let their college kids go south for spring break. I considered sprinkling a little sand in her bed and shower to add atmosphere here where The Old Folks are At Home; I reconsidered two days into her silent martyrdom. Being the "only one" not in Florida was no laughing matter, I was informed.

Surely, I worried, there was a way to express admiration for her diligence in hunting for a summer job (as opposed to suntan and beach boys) on spring break.

An early lesson learned at many a mother's knee is that if you're happy, go shopping to celebrate; sad, go shopping to cheer up; worried, go shopping to be distracted; disappointed, go shopping to be compensated.

It works.

And since I was in serious fashion trouble myself, I thought to kill two birds with one charge card. Maybe she could help me find something to wear to be at least partially "in" without being all the "way out."

She took the bait.

We'd been in only two teen specialty stores before my calculations totaled a staggering bottom line: It would've been cheaper to send her to Florida. My own fashion woes lay forgotten and crumpled like so much lint in the bottom of my purse. It's even harder trying to dress a teenager than a middling mom, I quickly discovered.

Top dollar is what it takes to be properly stylish in clothes I thought looked vaguely familiar as we scanned the racks dangling instant teen popularity. Somewhere I'd just seen such a shirt as daughter was modeling before a three-way mirror. Prewashed, acid-eaten, and triumphantly permanently wrinkled, it had a ripped shoulder seam and patches on the back. On purpose. In it, she looked just slightly overdressed for changing the oil or cleaning the gutters. Which, I suddenly remembered, was where I'd noticed a similar outfit: under the car.

When questioned, she, too, remembered the same old, old worn out shirt favored by our resident fix-it man. Slowly, a gleam of purpose shone from her eyes. Quickly hanging up the offending expensive "copycat" shirt, she led the way from the store in pursuit of an "original." We fled the mall, partners again, for home.

We upended the rag bag, garage sale-save sacks, and the mending basket onto the living room floor. Digging through the mounds of old clothes, she unearthed fashion treasures one after another. And look, she boasted, they will match her shoes—vintage three-year-old, gray, once-suede boots with holes in the back, soles, and sides. When questioned about the possibility of replacing them, she was scandalized. Why, only last week, she spluttered, a girl had offered to buy them.

Properly put in my place, I bemoaned again the paradox of sending children to college to develop their own interests, lives, and careers. All they do is "get ideas." I have only myself to blame for encouraging her, though, and shouldn't have been surprised at her style: she's an anthropology-archaeology major and loves old things.

But that's why, when she—wearing a nineteen-year-old shirt, twenty-seven-year-old sweater, and thirty-four-year-old coat atop those boots—gave me a big hug at the airport on her way north, I knew she was sincere.

Even though I didn't subsidize a Florida vacation and was still standing around in last season's threads myself, she confessed with a grin that from time to time I'm still one of her favorite old things.

Prayer

We miss our rites of passage, Lord, as we try to keep up with the next one. Always a fad behind, we chase the elusive image, flashed before us from slick pages, of who we would like to be. Or who we are told we would be happier being.

How are we to decide which is the real us? Which "look" should we pursue, our checkbooks out and ready to pay the price? Why is it so important for us to look like everybody else? Didn't you create us all different, and beautifully different at that?

Help me look in the three-way mirror of your expectations, your acceptance, your delight of me and see reflected a solitary, not one-of-a-crowd person who is adequate just as I am.

Do you laugh, or sigh in exasperation, when we sing

that hymn "Just as I am"? What irony; while we are singing along, we are looking around to see who else is better, who else we would like to be. A new, improved and updated version. Why do we reject ourselves, these selves who are cared about by you, right down to every hair on our heads?

Help us to accept who we are, this year's model of us, just as we are. Help us to change only those things, those inner things, that keep us from feeling as beautiful as you created us in the beginning.

Help us to put our checkbooks back in our pockets, rejecting sleek, outer images that can only cover the least important parts about us. Help us to look into the places where we need to revamp ourselves: our attitudes, our generosities, our commitments, our ethics.

Help us to hesitate before buying new images hung like garments on the rack to create somebody we aren't, and don't need to be, and to remember that we don't have to dress up to impress you. For surely you meant it when you promised that we are good enough to be your children, silly and vain though we may be, just as we are.

29

Hands Full of Life

The most beautiful pictures in my family scrapbook are a set of X ray mammography and ultrasound prints. Although black and white, they add color to my life, a dazzling kaleidoscope of images about what might've been and what can yet be.

Their high-technology scribblings and shadows were translated into action by a breast diagnostic center radiologist who advised that the lump in my right breast needed further evaluation. His advice and explanations accompanied praise for the prompt attention I'd given to an unwelcome intruder, a thief in the night. For I, like most women, had found my own lump. It was ice in the mind.

Until that moment, I thought I knew myself.

A small rubbery lump, however, introduced someone new: a frightened ostrich who longed to bury her head in the sands of a busy schedule, reciting all the while, "This can't be happening to me."

But it can and did.

Dialing the phone for the first appointment was hardest. After that, I took my head out of the sand for a closer look. Perhaps vision's a bit clearer for those of us who sport bifocals and must squint a little to see just how things really are. We've glimpsed that good life on over the hill and we want to reap the rewards of youthful efforts waiting there.

Diligent self-care is a small price to pay for a full ride toward those days of the rest of our lives, regardless of what we encounter. It may be only an interruption, a temporary roadblock. And so, last week, accompanied by a surgeon, I detoured through outpatient surgery.

The operating room gleamed, a fantasy in blue and bright, bright white, as the surgical team gathered in my honor about 2:40 P.M., my husband left behind to watch the clock.

Significant and comforting in its unexpectedness in that chilly place was the respect extended me, a scared but curious person, not a surgical site or number at all. Friendly touches and voices, explanations of procedures (surgical area scrubbed with amber antiseptic, cardiogram electrodes attached, IV begun) bridged the gap between that faraway locker where my belongings waited and the mysterious world of the patient.

A split-second sting, then another, of local anesthetic and I was under the knife, alert but sedated and uncaring about the rapid removal of the intruder, my ticket into this pungent, antiseptic world. The anesthetist and I chatted about the local football team, his medical future, and what was happening to me as I responded to his delicate balance at the controls of sedation.

"It's okay—a benign fibroid tumor," the surgeon announced, a pathology report confirming this within minutes.

Not a thief at all, merely an intruder. A nothing.

I clutched the good news to my lightly bandaged bosom on the way to the recovery room where I retrieved my energy. Shivering from the chilly operating room and the barren, frigid cave of fear where I'd lived for days, I relaxed beneath a warm blanket and parting words of the anesthetist, "It's over now." Soon I was untangling socks, a nurse buttoning my shirt.

Slush is beautiful. A salt- and grime-caked car is a magic chariot to carry me home by 5:30 P.M. to embrace breakfast dishes and dusty furniture, treasured relics of a busy life.

Pain? Very little. An occasional twinge as if I'd raked leaves too long. But then, no surgeon's scalpel can inflict more pain than the sharp edge of terror that had jabbed me for days.

Weariness, letdown, slight tenderness, and little swelling and discoloration are my only leftovers. And renewed vigilance. While a breast biopsy can't really be done during a lunch hour, it can in an afternoon, a life-saving way to spend time. It is, really, no big deal; to not do it, frequently is.

And my beautiful mammography prints? On file with my doctor, they are the first of a series to be taken every couple of years or so and then annually.

Probably I'll go on my birthday, my gift to myself. Then a toast, "Many happy returns of my day. May there be many more."

Prayer

Why me, Lord? Why me?

I raise my fist to you in defiance if this is your will. I found a lump in my breast today, Lord, slippery and terrifying in its eruption beneath my arm. My fingers can't leave it alone, and I've been in the bathroom most of the afternoon checking to see if it's still there. It is, it is, Lord. Why me?

This prayer is becoming a diary instead, for I can only write the beginning, I am so angry and scared. Can I have some space? I'm afraid to show you my rage and terror, afraid that you will be disappointed in me and my lack of faith. If I turn away from you in anger, will you be vanished when I turn back? I hope not, for I am alone enough already. But I can't bear to face you now in my rage, or in the arrogance I feel that I should be spared. Can I have some space?

Why me, Lord? Why me?

I raise my hand to you in petition. Reach out and grab my hand, hold it between yours so that I can feel your warmth, for I have none of my own. I was lonely and turned away from you in anger, with only my reflected fears to talk to. Are you there? Help me to forgive myself for mistakenly thinking the distance was you leaving me, when I was the one turning away. Forgive me for thinking I must be perfect—no lumps, no ugly moods—before I sought you. I need your support on this mile, Lord, even if you don't like the whining, crying person I am inside, for if I have you to talk to, I can spare my family this awful burden. Be with me tomorrow; be with the doctors; be with my husband, who would take my place if he could. Stay with him as he waits. Be with us both if I must relinquish a part of me that has both nourished and delighted.

Why me, Lord? Why me?

I raise my hand in victory, not because the lump was okay but because I am. How do I know I am okay? Because even in the midst of my fury, my self-pity and begging, my blame and defeat, you never gave up on me. I felt you in the parking lot, in the operating room. I saw you in the eyes of my doctor, the arms of my husband. I saw you not ever turn away from my ugliness of attitude and feeling of contamination of body invaded by an evil sore.

And now, O Lord, I ask you this time from my knees, Why me? What is there that you need me to do, now that I've been spared? Show me the job, the place, the people, where I can at last learn in my willingness to go with you.

Why me?

30

Tug-of-War

I don't know where the moon is today, but back when it was in the "seventh house, and Jupiter was aligned with Mars," women's issues seemed a lot simpler. It was all possibility, potential, and the euphoric sense of freedom school children have when bursting through the doors for recess.

The turbulent sixties, as history has since labeled them, were the musical dawning of the Age of Aquarius as well as the age of opened eyes. Women's opened eyes.

Shall we? Can we? Dare we? These were the questions unraveling the carefully stitched seams of our lives that we'd never corporately examined so closely before.

Quick upon the heels of those brave women who challenged ("Why?") traditional roles as the only roles open to women came those who went a step or two farther and dreamed ("Why not?") of attempting whatever they wanted and urging us to follow suit.

It was a time of battle: burning bras, storming "male bastions of power," and marching in solidarity, or what passed as solidarity in those days, for it appeared as if all the "sisters" yearned for the new day dawning.

150

Twenty years later, on the cusp of yet another moon, this one of the nineties, battle continues to rage between predictable and surprisingly unpredictable adversaries.

Men's amazement, and some discomfort, at the emergence of women as persons with equal skills and needs was predictable. Upset apple carts are never convenient, and usually someone trips over the spillage.

Women's polarization was unpredictable, at least to me as I blithely puttered along my way toward a career. It was a goal, like a clearing in the forest, I never consciously sought, to the amazement of my daughters who came along in time to see me as a role model.

"For what?" I sometimes still ask, perplexed at their intensity, their chomping at the bit to get on with "it."

Women, particularly young women, have charts, graphs, reams of articles, projections, time lines, lifelines and one-liners to guide them through the "jungle out there." Optimum times to advance corporately, maritally, maternally, and socially are plotted like so many points on a spreadsheet of life that looms before them as rigidly and grimly as any gender oppression their predecessors encountered.

From the strident seventies through the have-it-all, me-first eighties, we've gained momentum until we've come full circle to those first questions of the sixties: Who am I? What do I want?

Instead of taking twenty years to learn how to choose, which was what I celebrated in the beginning of the women's movement, have we only exchanged one kind of bondage for another? Self-appointed watchdog groups sit in judgment on one another, mandating "Truth" from opposite sides of issues: child care, ERA, parental leaves, birth control, abortion.

Choice seems an endangered concept, for those who do choose—on either side of an issue—find themselves criticized and challenged. If a woman stays home to care for young children, is she a dropout? Is she being ungrateful for not taking advantage of the place in line that has been "saved for her" by militant sisters on the cutting edge? Is one who works abandoning her nature, her instincts?

Today's woman is floundering in a unisex world between old and new role expectations. We long to understand what this abundant life is about, really. What kind of marriages should we build? What kind of family? What will we have to trade for what else? Are gains worth the costs? Do we dare admit that, no, they are not? How do we evaluate the inevitable tradeoffs?

We long for the good old days even as we strain to create the future, from vocations to sexuality. Blessing or curse, our womanhood: how are we to respond to God's gift of it? How do we respond to the male response to our newness, our emerging wholeness? Can we offer assurances that to be fully woman is to be fully needful of the fully male, that perhaps both can meet in new, more creative, faithful ways?

Yet another riddle of faith is taking place on our kitchen stoops. There must be directions to go, peace to make—even among the factions of women themselves—to be legacies for our daughters.

As I contemplate the nineties, a decade hardly more than a twinkle in the eye so far, I think of them as the not-quite nineties: we are not quite who we were once nor who we are yet to become as modern women. It will be a decade when we can become content with having not quite all of everything we thought we could have, when we will relegate the role of super woman to the back of our closets like last season's hemlines.

In the nineties fax and modems are already combining with the inherent rebellion of women as they "wake up and smell the coffee" of being exploited by both business and band wagons. It is a decade when the business world will come home. A decade of truce, too, perhaps, as we calm our shrill voices raised against one another across picket lines, political debates, and grocery store lines in battles over choices and who gets to decide for whom.

Like smoke from so many battle cannons, tendrils rose from our wiener-roast fire last week. Sufficiently stuffed with sizzling smoked sausages, baked beans, and potato salad, we languished around the embers picking at our marshmallow-sticky fingers and the question of what will it mean to be a woman in the nineties.

Guests for dinner around the fire pit in our yard were our youngest daughter and a friend who'd driven home from college to spend a few days of their fall break. These two young women, one an anthropology, the other a tele-communications major, are also women's studies minors and hold demanding, administrative campus jobs. Eloquently, they reject cold and unemotional role models as fiercely as they reject the unclad and air-headed or demure, passive ones held up as typical women by the advertising and entertainment media.

They and their peers march, they protest, they debate, they study and explore possibilities with a heartbreaking seriousness for the right of women to choose what is right for themselves in all areas. The greatest triumph, flickering like a coal in our campfire, is that frequently they do all these along with their male peers.

The day they left to return to campus, I went to the grocery store to replenish our depleted cupboards, still lost in my thoughts of these fascinating young women. Turning the corner at the frozen foods' section, I watched in startled discomfort as a young woman stepped in front of her shopping cart to shield her gurgling baby daughter, nestled amidst the potato chips, cereals, and cat food, from the approach of another woman.

153

I knew them both, having recorded as a reporter their equally fervent and thoughtful remarks delivered at a meeting where they represented opposite sides of an important issue: health, AIDS, and sex education in the public schools. Both felt their way was the best one to preserve the family.

Of ages just right for a three-generation spread of experience, the three females reached a stalemate by the frozen orange juice. Alienated, they stared at one another across a chasm of differences of opinion that threaten to divide them and us farther than we ever were before "women's lib." All the older woman appeared to want was to admire the baby, the younger woman to protect her baby from the older woman's contaminating radical ideas.

It remains to be seen what the baby wants: she's got some difficult choices ahead of her. Maybe by the time she's ready to ponder them, another line in that song from the past insistently rambling through my thoughts today will have come true: "and peace will guide the planets."

Not a chance, however, until we women retrieve those best parts of ourselves that have forever been true: nurturing, arbitrating, relating, comforting, teaching, creating. And, at the same time, not despising those other parts of ourselves: the fighting, foraging, defending, building, discovering, and designing that settled the American frontier, navigated migrations cross-country, cross-continents, advised kings in battle; invented Liquid Paper, disposable diapers and baby carriers, drip coffee, chocolate chip cookies, penicillin, rabies and meningitis serums and vaccines, voice-controlled wheelchairs, COBOL computer language, refrigeration, space helmets, cotton gin, and Apgar Scores; and discovered radioactivity, nuclear fission, DNA molecules, and X and Y chromosomes.

Homemaking, invention-making, baby-making, corporate merger-making, peacemaking. We women have always been good with the "doing" verbs.

Prayer

My favorite color should be plaid, Lord. I can't decide much of anything these days as easily and simply as some think I should. The issues aren't as clear-cut as they might at first appear.

Tugged and pulled, I scramble to keep up with the emerging puzzle of being a woman. What do you think about a woman vice president? President? Biological clocks? Child care? Equal rights? Discrimination? How should I feel?

More than anything, Lord, I envy the certainty of those convinced their way is right and that that way is your way. I'm not so sure that is true, Lord, and I see others about me unconvinced, too.

How strange and sad that some of our biggest battles are among the sisters. You'd think, Lord, that as mothers, at least by nature, we'd know that each child is different, unique, and to be developed individually.

Yet, too often I feel confined, judged, restricted, and angered by current attitudes. The rivalry for being your handmaiden is fierce!

Give us some clarity, a broader vision, more tolerance of sisters unwilling to claim their own lifestyles, willing to remain dominated. And tolerance for those who do select a direction we might not understand.

For those of us who seek to combine our roles, help us to find realistic yardsticks to measure our successes at juggling it all. Ease our discontent when we're at home and not at the office and vice versa, Lord.

Give us compassion for those who bear the weight of social change and new approaches that jolt us from middle-class smugness and complacency. Guard us from insisting on simplistic solutions to complex problems as if to will a lifestyle, to want something, is to create it.

Give us energy and sustain our time-proven tenacity to bring about positive change for those women who have no choices: victims of economy, brutality, poverty, illness, discrimination. Keep us uneasy in our own hard-won successes as long as there are any who have only failures and limits and no choices.

I'm changing again, Lord, and I want you to help me guard against the very rigidity I occasionally envy. Continue to let me see a multitude of possibilities for being a woman in your creation, a Mary or a Martha, a housewife or a lawyer. Equally sanctified and valuable. Equal choices.

Bless our diversity, Lord, and continue to let it flourish.

31

Happy New Year

My checking account is overdrawn only three days into the new year. An inkling of things to come? I would like to know, for it appears I need to amend my resolutions, broken already. I'd like to know about some other things as well, such as, how was last year, really? What have I got to build on?

January. Happy New Year time. A time when Janus, the two-faced Greek god of January, looks both forward and backward as we all do, hovering at the brink of the new year while contemplating the old.

Sunday was the day after the year before, the first one in another cycle of endings, beginnings, evolutions, and milestones. A new year, unknown, untried, is already upon us, from checking account overdrafts to resolutions already broken; from regrets brought with us to grandiose predictions.

We're seasoned futurists, having already passed 1984, the year that the future began. One of the most anticipated years in history, it was the year of Orwellian conjecture. Truth or fiction, it nonetheless ushered us into a futuristic turn of a century already in its waning phase.

Lodged in the toe of my son's Christmas stocking

with an orange and a candy cane was a copy of *Future Almanac,* a gift fought over by young and old alike after the turkey was dismembered. It predicted that New Year's party revelers of the future will wear body-clinging suits, which like all clothing then will be more functional to protect us against weather extremes. Are we seeing some of them now, I wonder, as I contemplate our drought-stricken county soaking up winter rains.

Sports will also be touched by the hand of progress as bionic athletes have surgery not for repair but for improvement. More and more athletes will have computer chips implanted in the brain to stimulate muscles for exercise; yellow and orange baseballs will follow trends set by golf balls and tennis balls. Families will arrive at these bionic sports events in computer-controlled cars, the better to avoid traffic and accidents, even at one-hundred-mile-per-hour speeds.

Don't want to ride? Take a moving sidewalk on one of the miles of "sidewalk highways." Trolly buses, the future's answer to mass transit, will be operated not by a whistling bus driver but by a computer with direction locaters. Space walks and exploration will become like the Old West, with space colonization an option.

But not all of us will be around to compare notes: The extinction of the whooping cranes, grizzly bears, whales, gorillas, and elephants is projected due to changing environments and pollution. Fellow survivors? Cockroaches, gulls, black bears, and penguins, according to forecasters.

Perhaps as insurance against some of these perplexing predictions—or fanciful tales—thoughts turn to "considering other alternatives," "turning the tide," "resolving to do better." For no matter how mind boggling is the time ahead, still synonymous with "New Year" is "resolution"—that annual attempt to stomp out unwanted habits, to create the best person, most peaceful world, cleanest house, and most efficient worker, all with the mere exertion of will power and a line or two scribbled on a piece of paper.

Sifting through a myriad of ideas, I've settled upon a resolutionary theme: self-care.

Houses can fend for themselves; dust and old magazines never hurt anyone. Worlds revolve themselves for the most part. Jobs carry their own momentum, reaching "max" efficiency in the face of doing what has to be done. "Selfs," though, need more care: so be it resolved to become physically fit, nutritionally savvy, spiritually awake, emotionally agile.

Overly simple resolutions for a complex year, for futuristic scenarios? Perhaps. Necessary, though, for fortifying and enabling us for the task ahead, the same task that has been ours since the first new year was rung in: living one day at a time into the wherever. Whether resolutions be personally generic or globally lofty, now is the time to effect change.

As we do, keep, like Janus, an eye behind to where our footprints have been, the other scanning the untrampled sands ahead. Both halves of the whole of change. For, "Life can only be understood backwards; but it must be lived forwards," observed Sören Kierkegaard, a Swedish theologian.

Same time next year. Only then can it be determined if this one indeed will have been a "Happy New Year."

Prayer

If we could see around the corner, Lord, would we really want to?

Might it not make us even more frantic to control everything—from the weather so it won't rain on our picnic to the price of September soybeans? Markets, marriage, and the mundane succumb to the methodical ticking of a clock, to our frustration, Lord, as you know so well from hearing our complaints.

But with a little foreknowledge can we better pre-pare for what awaits us like a great "Gotcha!" game? Might we be a little kinder to one another if we knew that someone would be moved away, even dead, by the spin of another New Year's sparkler?

Shouldn't we live as if the future is now, Lord, pro-tecting, nurturing, and saving our world, our families? Ourselves?

Each day is a gift, sufficient unto itself, you implore us to see. Blind, though, we insist on squandering today, putting off until tomorrow doing better, being better, following you better.

One reason we race pell-mell, Lord, is that we're afraid we won't get it all done, see it all, experience it all. And in our frantic rush to consume our allotment of days, we race right past the exquisite moment, like a snowflake, unlike no other and never to be retrieved.

Help me, Lord, with your clarity to guide me, to check back over last year. As if it were a buffet you spread before me, guide me in taking the best it had to offer into this empty table set for tomorrow.

Courage most of all, Lord, is what I need this time of year, not only to face what waits unseen ahead, but what remains behind. Be with me in a moment of con-fession for last year; let me name to you my sins and errors. Even though I went on, they remain trouble-some. And from this confession, inspire me to make amends.

Fortify me for the events that wait to drain me; spare any that may harm my family, Lord. Grant a good year to them, too. Strengthen my resolve to keep resolutions that will enable my life to be better; give me the com-mon sense to discard those that only add stress.

Here we stand at the turnstile of another year, Lord. I'm ready if you are.

32

Leftover Time

She crunched ice, chomp, chomp, until I thought I would scream. All night long.

A forgivable annoyance, I finally decided around dawn. Her delivery had been long; her thirst was unquenchable.

Mine was, veteran that I appeared to be. I had beat her to our due dates by five days. Now complications (my infant son was ill) were keeping me tethered to the hospital. The nurses and pediatrician, sympathetic to my frustration, arranged for us to share a room.

My spirits lifted the minute she was wheeled into my room. No more whining, I promised the nurse, who smiled her approval of that, sure enough. True to my word, I was soon laughing despite the ice crunching, which became a "family joke." She was my best friend.

Best friends—soul sisters, we used to claim on our shared southern heritage. Together we shuffled to the nursery, took turns admiring and holding one another's babies, and dreamed great dreams of their growing up best friends, as we were.

Which we were and remained long past the days when my son and her third daughter, those squalling nursery mates, quit toddling together; long past the days when our families picnicked together; long past the days when it seemed forever away that we would grow old gracefully together, which we planned from the arrogant, distant surety of our youth.

Best friends. "Like sisters," she cried when I had to move from the neighborhood and eventually the state.

An absence of daily contact diluted our assumptions of friendship during the intervening years, but we kept in touch.

At five minutes past the engraved starting time, the guests, not to mention the minister and organist, were fidgety several years ago during her second daughter's wedding by the time I slipped into my pew, the mother of the bride on my heels.

As she passed my pew, few made the connection or saw our conspiratorial wink confessing the reason: our impromptu reunion in the back hall. We'd met unexpectedly in a covey of bridesmaids just as the organ began its summons. Late as usual, I'd come in the wrong door of the unfamiliar church. Sending the bridesmaids scooting ahead, we'd clung to each other in mutual support for our new roles as parents of adult children, of brides so soon.

If, as our hug assured, we'd survived the 2 A.M. feedings, toddlers, teething, braces, first loves, broken limbs, drivers' licenses, and rock music required of us by our seven children, surely we could survive anything.

Survive.

Maybe she will; surely she will, for reports are encouraging.

A difference between us greater than the miles between our homes now is that she put off going to the doctor when she found a breast lump; I didn't. Mine was benign; hers was not.

Seven lymph nodes had taken advantage of her hesitancy, her spring busy-ness, her job deadlines taking priority. Spring days raced pell-mell into summer and fall, keeping frantic pace with the cancer growing within her left breast, which by now "looked funny."

Weekly chemotherapy drains her irrepressible energy, the dread of it her bubbly optimism. Not doing it is never considered. "For very long," she corrects.

Oh, my friend, how could you not go to the doctor? Why did you allow this to happen to you, to me? For I am the more vulnerable knowing that if you are such easy prey to this obscenity, this thief in the night, I must surely be.

The more things change, the more they stay the same, and once again my friend, accompanied now by a husband of thirty years, is surrounded by children: four lovely grown daughters, two grandchildren, and another expected on its grandfather's birthday.

The years telescope against my will, and I see her as I once knew her: making apple pies from fresh-picked fruit, a litter of kids underfoot; sewing frilly dresses for little girls and their dolls to match; hanging wallpaper—crooked—in an old house with not one level wall; plowing a field and dancing until midnight all on the same day. A remarkable person.

Most of all, though, she's a best friend. And what, my friend, are we going to do about all those plans to grow old together? It's not time, it's not time, is all I can say. We haven't finished being friends.

Prayer

Are you with her in that chilled, chilling place as they thread needles into her veins? Are you with her, holding her head and wiping it with a cool cloth during hours of retching violence? Are you with her in the morning hours just before dawn when the worst fears seem bound to come true?

I need to be there, but can't. Divorce reroutes more

than marriage boundaries, and I am unwelcome by too many in that town, by those who would begrudge me my place at her side. So, be there for me when I can't be. Let memories of our escapades, our shopping marathons, our late-night cups of tea, our casual joy with one another's presence, flow through her veins along with the life-restoring medicine. Can you let me be a channel of your healing in such small ways? I'm willing.

Teach me wisdom to judge how close I can be to her without crowding the life she's made without me. Forgive me for resenting those who claim her now with casseroles and cards, when I should be the one she can lean on. Help me forgive myself for being glad, on the other hand, that I'm not there daily to be ground down, down, down into despair in the face of statistics and her anguish.

I'm a coward, Lord, and I don't want to have to face all this, especially the part that reminds me of my own vulnerability. I'm selfish, too, and I am uncomfortable with my own good fortune, with my smug feelings of having been so vigilant. Help me to understand that you want healing and wholeness for both of us, all of us; that you didn't choose me or her to be either afflicted or spared; that illness happens.

Help me most of all to focus on your promises of companionship through the dark valleys filled with shadows of many sorts, whether they be on X ray films or not. Remind me again and again that I am being a channel for your healing power in the silly cards I send, the impromptu phone calls, the newsy notes. And if you need me to do more, send me.

33

Silver Ribbons

Moles, we squinted in sudden sunlight as the train chugged out of Chicago's cavernous Union Station. The skyline hurried in the opposite direction as we gathered speed toward our westward destination.

All aboard at last.

We had a daughter to visit at Ghost Ranch, New Mexico, a working ranch and church conference center. Prospects of a few days with her prompted us to put deed to thought, for this was a spot we'd always wanted to see. But 3,000 miles worth of motel rooms and sacks of fast food, not to mention trauma to our car already weary with 140,000 miles under its belts, lay between here and there. Air fare kept us grounded, and renting a car still didn't eliminate eating and showering on the road. Our dream was sidetracked.

Traveling by train never entered my mind, for I thought the majestic iron horses were dead. But, according to information that found its way to my littered desk, the trusty steeds have only been sleeping, being roused today by folks like us. I called, as the brochure invited, for more information.

The other children, teenagers, hadn't known they

165

wanted to ride the rails, but were intrigued in spite of having to travel with parents.

I'd always been fascinated with trains, having enjoyed small jaunts as a child to visit relatives. We would chug out of town behind an engine pulling us, back into town ahead of an engine pushing us. Asking my grandfather for the correct time on his gold railroadman's pocket watch guaranteed a story about his early years as a hobo when trains were trains, he sighed.

How marvelous to hop a fast freight, a magic carpet, I yearned when I was a child mired in homework, piano lessons, and walking the dog.

Years later, it still seemed a good idea, and I found the next best thing: a caboose to make into a cozy home. They were for sale, castoffs orphaned like derelicts along big-city sidings. Yours for the hauling and decorating, cabooses were a momentary fad in those eclectic times, and I settled for a railroad lantern, its red and blue bull's-eye windows casting a nostalgic glow over dinner party conversation.

Although computers operate trains today, conductors still help you up the steps, and tea still sloshes over cup rims if you're not careful. We sliced through dusk in the heartland, past cows gossiping over fences; past portable signs selling fireworks and salvation; past boarded-up churches and soldout softball games.

We roved like census takers, nodding to fellow passengers, many of them young families complete with dolls, cars, games, and bedtime snacks. Senior citizens, Boy Scouts, and commuters filled the cars to capacity. A community on wheels, we were connected to our journey as we swayed and rocked down the narrow lines. Our bones savored the vibrating miles clicking off beneath us like kids skating over sidewalk cracks; on a train, all senses are taking the trip.

Frequent whistle stops punctuated dreams from beneath the blankets we'd brought, and moldering

grain elevators, factories, and neon-lit diners that could only belong trackside crept up on Kansas until it, too, flickered drowsily past. Until dawn.

I squinted at the same station sign I'd seen the last time I'd awakened, and the time before that. We were stopped. Suddenly the conductor strode purposefully through the car reversing his traditional instructions. "Everybody off."

A track washout on our scheduled route through Colorado was detouring some passengers onto buses to complete their journeys. Having changed our itinerary at the last minute, we were not affected and yawned gratefully into a pre-breakfast snooze lullabied by the repetitious songs the train sang for itself as we hurried by houses that trembled before us, traffic that obeyed.

Waffles and tea were savored in Oklahoma, miles south of where we were supposed to be on this alternate route, a bonus as far as I was concerned. Waving grain, spacious skies, dust storms, cowboys, antelope, and sagebrush flashed by like lines in the national anthem.

We were now on freight, not passenger, tracks, and as we roamed through the backyards of America's towns, we sped past junk yard after junk yard, those national monuments erected to obsolescence. We wound past the bleached bones of the Detroit Cougar, Mustang, Lynx, and Bobcat; beside the abandoned carcasses of iceboxes, televisions, and washers felled by the lure of newer models.

A cleansing view of mountains appeared on the horizon over a quick peanut-butter-and crackers lunch.

New Mexico.

Bring boots, our daughter had advised. In July? I'd questioned. For the rattlesnakes, she calmly replied. I pulled mine on before the train whistled to a stop in a majestic land of colliding cultures.

Piñon pine, cedar, red, red rocks to climb; crisp, thin air to inhale deeply; ancient cliff dwellings; Indian wisdom and lore; a starlit, firelit gathering in an adobe home once occupied by artist Georgia O'Keefe.

A magic-carpet ride.

Too soon, the train whistle summoned us: time to punch the return tickets.

Up, up and over the Colorado mountains, the train labored on the repaired tracks, boulders and mud still visible from the slide that had detoured us. Union Station hadn't missed a beat in the rhythm of life while we were gone; nor had home, where life is viewed in still-life watercolors, not murals unfolding reel upon reel.

Riding the rails was a treasure wrapped in the silver ribbons of track to be pasted between pages of memory.

Prayer

I've been to see your land, Lord. Marvelous, marvelous. And I could've kept right on churning with that big silver engine until I reached the sea, then turning like a swimmer, pushed off the wall and headed for the other sea.

You have given us such a mixture of sights, Lord, in this chunk of world I claim for my national allegiance. Sights, smells, sounds, sensations.

And stinking garbage.

Like a spy, Lord, I peered on the other side of the fences from the train window, and I saw the secret.

Oh, Lord, what are we thinking when we pile our leftover fads behind corrugated walls? That these rusting screens are hiding anything? That fenders and hubcaps, refrigerators, trucks, sinks and tubs, water heaters and furnaces, wads of foil, bales of crushed yellow school buses, and tons of slag will softly crumble under gentle rains into fodder for the soil?

How stupid we are. Or how willful, Lord. We want it, use it, toss it, and forget it; out of sight, out of mind.

It's as if trash is invisible, and we duck our heads in embarrassment if we come unexpectedly face to face with it, like meeting an old friend grown dowdy, or worse yet, drunk and disorderly. Disgusted, we disconnect from the unlovely.

We lay no claim to the waste, human and industrial, that washes on our shores; we are innocent of the litter sown with dandelion-like abandon along our highways; we are shocked at the floating barges that have no place to unload garbage. Someone else's garbage, Lord, certainly not ours.

For we don't make garbage. At least, we amend, those tremendous stockpiles of rat-and-disease havens that border the back sides of train tracks. Those were created by huge corporations, giant cities, enormous factories, we explain. And isn't it shameful, we mutter dolefully, shaking our heads in dismay.

You know, though, don't you, Lord, where it all begins?

A clue, Lord, it's the same place it can end, actually

169

the only place it can ever end: in a single candy bar wrapper. And a single car, a single disposable diaper, a single tire, even a single chewing gum wrapper. No matter how small it is, Lord, when each tiny thing is tossed by each one of us standing at the edge of a single garbage pit, it overflows.

My land runneth over, Lord.

If it is to be reclaimed, Lord, into any kind of world we would want to have dominion over, make us smell our own garbage; force our noses into the stench. Press our nearsighted eyes against a hole in the corrugated camouflage fences until we see that unless we recycle, conserve, and plan, this heap will keep growing until it, not vacation routes, will spread from sea to shining sea.

God, shed your grace on us so that we will have time, like errant children, to clean up the mess we have made in our own living room.

34

Overdrawn

Tax forms arrived in the same bundle of mail as did my overdrawn notice from the bank. Will I ever get ahead? Better question, how will I ever know?

I round off my checkbook to the nearest sawbuck, calling it even if the bank and I more or less agree. Bookkeeping for me is simple: outgo always exceeds income.

There's never enough to back up the checks it takes to fuel, feed, tread, and educate three kids. Don't forget dogs to dip and distemper, or colds and flus to treat, gifts and donations to supply, movies to see—cheap matinee movies. It's hard to keep track of where it all goes. My longest ledger column is "H.O.K.," heaven only knows!

Oh, for the good old days when life was simpler, essentials cheaper.

Good old days when an acquaintance was born, a century ago. The drinking straw was invented the year of her birth, 1888. So were the camera, electric streetcars, and the adding machine, according to birthday trivia cranked out of a computer to be made into a birthday card. Survivors were gathering at Gettysburg for a twenty-fifth anniversary; "Casey at the Bat" was published; and the Washington Monument was completed.

How times have changed in the checkbook realm as well. A loaf of bread cost a nickel, and I can't think what that will buy today. Milk cost a quarter, then. The first folks to gather 'round black-and-white television sets about 1928 paid the same as their heirs do today; color, about four times as much.

The first coast-to-coast telephone calls cost $22.50 for three minutes; today direct calls average less than $3.

As the present becomes today's past, with most of us too busy to do more than hurry to catch up, what then of the future? If I can't balance my checkbook and manage a budget now, how can I spiral upward along with costs of living? And what if I don't want to give up my standard of living?

Two penny-pinching shopping companions were behind me in line last week at the grocery store. Examples of frustration, named like items on their grocery lists, floated to me in cartoon balloons over their generic staples and cost-cutter sale items.

Waiting impatiently for the slow line to move, I unashamedly listened in on their woes: mortgages, retirement, their parents' care, college, braces. Even finding money for next week's grade-school lunches was worrisome.

It made for sorry eavesdropping, but I was caught between our similarities as much as our carts. None of us was at poverty level, but we sounded near destitution. Like paint-by-number drawings, tough financial realities have become the lines within which people are carefully coloring their lives in red tones of frustration and drab grays of boredom. Few of us, though, are willing or content to stay within these or any boundaries. We resist diets, curfews, and budgets. We drive where and when we want. We want to be and have the best at work and play.

Slaves to pleasure, as the sociologists are fond of calling us these days, we are frantic for fun. Expecting no boredom, good weather, and 300-horsepower motors, we lament our lot when broke or bored. Or overdrawn. Spectators of life, we substitute speed for achievement and passive viewing for fun, a newscaster recently accused.

Surely not me, I thought smugly, distancing myself from the whiners behind me. I just get a little over-extended from time to time; there are, after all, things one must have. Usually on sale, I preened.

Nothing serious; no chronic dis-ease, and I could balance my account if I wanted to. I could be content, for I still am captain of my own ship, so to speak, albeit it has 134,001 miles and no gas. But, yes, I resent its rusted limitations.

Guiltily, I surveyed my shopping cart idling before me. There it was, prepackaged gourmet, substitute cooking as warned. Speed—less than twenty minutes for a three-course meal—substitute achievement. All I have to do is punch two buttons, throw paper napkins on the table and yell, "Dinner's served." Quickie eating: substitute dining.

Could there be a connection between my cart and my checkbook? Maybe.

For I, like many, have cruised down the bucolic lanes of our past carefree lives headed for a change of scenery, a little break in routine whenever I wanted. In constant need of diversion, I-we have overeaten, over-spent, and overentertained.

"If only" has become a favorite phrase as "wants" exceed "haves" at our house, one among many in the neighborhood of the world. From there it's not a far leap to "musts," a place where problems arise, frustrations increase, and resentments form. Counselors point out that more marriages are in trouble over money than sex or in-laws.

Suspicions abound as we wonder if we're getting our

fair share, or honest now, if others are getting more than theirs. We compare, compete, and complain about the Joneses who are always a step ahead.

Why couldn't we instead compete, one of our greatest pastimes from spelling bees to football games, toward a new set of goals: the smallest utility bill, the best mileage, the most economical recipe, the simplest homemade meal? Like first graders patiently learning new skills, surely we can drive past our overflowing landfills of luxury, monuments to our disposable society, and realize we need to change some habits, I thought as I exchanged three days' worth of work for two sacks of groceries.

Yet supper was not in either of them: that night was traditionally pizza-delivered-in night. This computes to a morning's worth of work if we all get large soft drinks and every topping, except anchovies, on the pizza. Pizzas plural: we eat a lot.

Putting away the groceries, having the pizzas ordered and a more-or-less rubber check written and waiting for them, I stood indicted, fast food on the way, foil in one hand, paper plates in the other.

A far cry from another kitchen.

In my grandparents' dimly lit and wonderfully pungent pantry was a huge bowling-ball sized sphere of foil. Carefully constructed over many months, it was smoothed and formed against the day "we might need it." On the pantry shelves there were also skeins of string, scraps of wrapping paper, pencil nubbins, and a soap saver in which to reuse soap scraps.

A step backward could be a step forward. That's the choice, the challenge: Can less become more?

Prayer

I charged new jeans today, Lord, and a new sweater and some socks. But I needed the jeans; the girls the other stuff. All the way home, I felt I was running faster than the car was driving: anxiety, Lord. Guilt.

Don't make me have to give up anything, Lord. Quit shoving pictures of starving children or homeless people under my nose. It spoils my appetite.

Pardon the sarcasm, Lord, but I am so frustrated with trying to decide how to live in a world of such extremes. From my little patch of ground in the middle of them, I'm hanging on to the good life for all I'm worth. Which, by the way, in this country is a lot more than elsewhere—another uncomfortable fact, for how can one person be more valuable than another?

Yes, why do I deserve what I have, and another woman in another place has not even a percentage point of it? Is it chance, luck, preordained, or what, that she is there with a starving child with only a drought to break the monotony of famine, and I am here with my old car, the latest diet, two ovens and a grill to cook more food than she sees in a year?

Forgive me, Lord, and I ask her forgiveness as well, that I'm not willing to change my life, at least not without a fight. Thank you for the first round this afternoon as I eavesdropped on my own selfishness at the store.

I don't promise much, Lord, for I am so slow to change. Please give me time to adapt to new ways.

Hold off the impending disastrous message I can hear gaining volume in the growing wails of hunger from my neighbors, near and distant. Hold it off until I can prepare myself by cutting down a little at a time.

How selfish is even this plea, that I be given time when many have none; that I be given a reprieve in which to enjoy my second helpings of the good life.

Spare your anger, Lord; withhold your disgust as I drop pennies in the pails of the needy.

Quickly, Lord, for I am beginning to feel an urgency, help me figure out what to do. I will do it, I promise, without first asking if even doing so little will matter.

It will, Lord, it will, it will. For I suddenly see that it is not only that others need to get from me but I need to give.

Look at my hands, Lord, held out before me. See how they curl back on themselves in order to hold on to what I have. Hands, Lord, that are in great danger of losing their ability to reach out to others, to you.

Open them, Lord; help me learn to save in order to give.

35

Passing the Buck

In this era of Watergates, Irangates, and Holygates, if I had a buck, I'd pass it on. I only wish I'd had one sooner.

For, once upon a sweltering Tennessee afternoon three months shy of my sixth birthday, I gave myself a haircut.

Neighborhood friends and I had worked all week building a hideout in the thick hedge behind my house. Humidity, like a great, gray elephant, squatted on my chest, and I couldn't breathe. Prickly-heat bumps on my neck erupted faster than water droplets on the bottles of cold soft drinks we swigged.

All week I'd complained about the long hair drooping down my back. It snagged in the bushes, unbraided itself, and gave me a headache when I tugged it back into a ponytail.

"I dare you!" Becky's challenge echoed through the greenly dim, damp hideout. "Yeah, cut it off," another urged.

I debated through a picnic of peanut butter sandwiches, hard-boiled eggs, and fresh sugar cookies my mother carried out to us in her wicker picnic hamper.

Later, squinting into a mirror held steady by a friend and coached by daredevil Becky, I lifted my long hair in one hand and sawed through it with the other, Mother's stolen sewing scissors intent on their task.

A six-year-old hank of hair soon covered my feet, exposing my neck to what breezes there were; jagged, short bangs fluttered suddenly uncertain above my worrying eyes.

My hair was supposed to stay long. I'd agreed to let it keep growing and was looking forward to a professional trim before first grade in the fall. But I was hot, the scissors handy, and Becky, visiting from New York, had the short, curly hairdo I wanted.

Bad news travels fastest, especially when carried by tattletales.

Watching from behind my mother, who'd come hunting me at the first hint of my haircut, stood the little snitch slowly licking a fudgesicle, piety and chocolate dripping down his chin.

During Mother's disappointment and anger, my punishment, a humiliating trip to the hairdresser, and the ensuing months waiting for my hair to recover, I focused on the snitch and Becky the tempter.

They had gotten me into Big Trouble.

"They made me do it," I protested with the eloquence of wronged virtue. "It's not my fault," I defended. "He shouldn't have snitched," I whined.

The worst punishment, worse than not being allowed to ride my new bike for a week or get ice cream from the pony-driven cart that clip-clopped daily through the neighborhood, was remembering the peanut butter sandwiches my trusting mother had brought to the hideout. For a long time, peanut butter stuck in my throat, extra gummy chunks of guilt.

For even longer, I savored blame and alibis: if the snitch had kept his mouth shut; if Becky had not dared me; if Mother had not been unreasonable about wanting my hair long; if August had not been so hot.

If, if, if. Then I would not have gotten into trouble.

Like presidents and their you-name-it-gate buddies.

Like candidates who dip their paddles into the wrong puddles. Publicly.

Like televangelists who divert widows' mites into their own pockets on prime time, or collect quickie sexual favors as offerings due in the plate.

Like all whose woes, apparently, are the results of exposure by the press, tips from snitches, and demands of the unreasonable public. Yes, unreasonable is that loyal public who believe they are buying a potion of religion, an hour of surrogate purity, from those who preach immunity to temptation and are true believers of their own press releases. Are those holders of public trust shocked at disapproval? Not as greatly, not as traumatically, as they are at getting caught.

Was I, years ago, as innocent, as "betrayed" as they? Think of the remorse I wasted. Think of all the peanut butter I could've enjoyed standing there in all my shorn glory and innocence! The seduction of alibis, first tried when Adam finger-pointed at Eve, hasn't lost its allure since then, to when I clutched the "smoking scissors" in my hand, and until today.

Popularity of "The devil made me do it" jokes and T-shirts a few years back is understandable: No one wants to be holding the buck when it stops.

But just plain 'fessing up is good for children, Mother gently insisted (if not for grown-up souls these days). We soon mended the troubles caused, I grudgingly admitted, by me.

Even yet sometimes my feet tickle as if covered by hanks of hair. You know the times, those moments of temptation to protest, "But, officer, traffic is going faster than I am." Or to promise, "The check's in the mail." Or to whine, "But everybody else does it." Or to bargain, "Hmmmm, no one will know."

But, hey, feet, stop worrying. Today's message just broadcast by the most recently spotlighted politico scoundrel and bad-boy preacher is that it wasn't my fault my hair got cut—it was Becky's for tempting me; Mother's for catching me; and the snitch's for tattling.

In journalism, that's called taking "literary license," you know, a little rewriting. Or in another case, it's a little tampering with the Good News, which is being changed to advise, "Take this buck and 'Pass it On.'"

Prayer

Lead us not into temptation? I always thought that meant like robbing banks, Lord, or shooting the neighbor's dog for keeping me awake. Or the neighbor.

Those are easy to resist. It's the other kinds of temptations that wait in ambush for me, such as the candy bars at the check-out counter, the ones that will gain me unwanted pounds, a headache, and guilt. Why, then, do I insist on checking to see if there are any new ones even though I've sworn off eating any, old or new? Temptation.

Such as the change that falls from the dispenser at

the same time as does my soda pop. Something for nothing. Will a quarter, dime, and nickel bankrupt the store? Aren't the costs for things outrageous, padded as they are? Why do I hesitate before giving the change to the clerk? Temptation.

Such as the sniffle that could be exaggerated into an excuse for not going to tonight's boring, boring meeting, What difference will one person's absence make anyhow? Why don't I learn instead to say no when first asked to do something I know I'll be trying to get out of? Temptation.

Such as not speaking up when what I have to say may be unpopular; such as blaming the other driver when I'm the one who crowded him; such as starting a rumor. Temptations.

Silly temptations, Lord, are they too petty to trouble you with? It is even a temptation to believe such a thing, Lord, so that I won't have to make the leap from petty to big, from occasional to habitual in the little discrepancies I create in my life.

Keep me staring at the chasm between what I say and what I do, Lord, so that I can see that your peace comes from your being consistent and from your not excusing my small sins because they aren't big. A lie is a lie is a lie.

Keep me uncomfortable, tug on my hair to get my attention if you have to, in order to remind me how silly it is for me to hide, to pass the buck. For, Lord, you see it all. You know so well how disobedient your children are. Which must be why you promised to be with us on our paths strewn with lovely, delectable, and alluring temptations from candy bars to casual sex, government cover-ups, and points in between.

Give us the good sense to understand how willingly we will partake of whatever we think we should have. Give us ears to hear our own hollow and glib justifications. Give us the humility to know we can't go through all the check-out lanes of life alone. Stay nearby.

36

Bark Louder than Bite?

What language is a bark?

An unseen dog vigorously announced my arrival for an interview, and the question waited on the porch with me for the door to open.

What language is a greeting?

A smile is about the only place to meet between cultures, and two strangers shared one over the differences spoken in my midwesternized Tennessee twang and her lilting Japanese.

Offered her nickname in place of her real one, I practiced until she nodded I'd gotten it right.

So far, the only wife to join her Japanese businessman-husband in our small town, she was my Thursday newsroom assignment. No one had mentioned a Japanese dog, especially one named for a famous American actor, and she laughed at my astonishment. I'd expected a classic Japanese word, such as the one I'd heard the week before when I'd met her at a Brownie Scout meeting. She was there to fold papers, Origami-style. I was there just doing a job. Her smile changed all that, and I wanted to know more than which line to fold to make a paper hat. I wanted to know how she would feel if I folded the only shape I know: the legendary peace cranes that commemorate regrets about igniting her country. I kept my hands in my pocket.

Today, as women on occasion find, conversation turned to food. Used to the question, she assured me that Japanese cooking is not what we're served in the United States. Here less than two months, she'd already invited a few new American friends to dinner, to discovery, to authenticity—she struggled with the word. It's an elusive word in any language, I assured her.

The genuine article, authentic beauty, I knew at a glance when she unfolded exquisite silk panels she'd created with an intricate dyeing process I wouldn't understand even if we landed on the right words. My mind, truant, skipped home and tried to decide what treasures I would take with me were I in her shoes. What could I not live without? An uncomfortable question, it brought my thoughts back to our conversation that was making me sweat. It is hard work to find the right words; some, we never did, simply substituting a smile, a shrug, or a laugh in its place. How much of what I say is really worth translating? I wondered, suddenly tongue-tied under the weight of my magpie chatter.

A natural teacher, she speaks, demonstrates what she is speaking about, and invites visitors to ask questions. Learning is an exchange of ideas, she explained, and I could imagine how her school students must miss her.

The silk panels, I finally understood, tell the tale of her patience and enjoyment of doing a task right. And with a smile, a characteristic she readily acknowledged. Taught as a child, she explained, that if you are kind you will be happy with yourself, which will make you smile, her face broke into another one at my surprise over such a simple explanation.

It is possible to keep smiling, she said, even in a new land with its different sounds, sights, foods, manners, and language. A land where already a few had gleefully used the language barrier to practice a little fraud, a big deception. Most, though, are kind, here, too, she added, not surprised at all, and I thought about the paper cranes. Have they forgiven us?

I learned later, after I left this gentle lady, there are those who've not forgiven her: treachery and mistrust, generation unto generation.

We joined forces, though, in a battle against fleas, tiny warriors that wear their skeletons like armor on the outside of their bodies. Her beloved dog, brought from Japan, she admitted shamefully, was itching terribly. I told her I thought any country without fleas must be lovely, and apologized for our infestations that are driving American pet owners crazy, too. Mental note: Stop at the store where she's been shopping to explain that they need to speak more slowly when advising her on treatment.

On another point, we agreed entirely: chili with beans is very good. A disagreement in counterpoint followed: She thinks American drivers are polite. I was astonished, promising her I'd look again.

When would she go home? Next fall, to sing, she answered, her face lighting up at the thought of a reunion with family left behind, to sing a special, noble song in a special theater just for this type of singing, which is only a hobby, she tried to tell me.

She is a lover of music, she confided, of all types of music, but especially the Negro spirituals, she added, tilting her head to recapture the melody of her favorite.

"Deep river . . ." she began, and unexpectedly we found ourselves singing together, humming through the measures where words were forgotten, where words were pronounced a little differently.

More than a deep river separates our two countries,

our histories, one another, and I held a note to blend with hers just that extra count. Had we found a bridge?

Prayer

"Jesus loves the little children, all the children of the world," we used to sing. And so do you. So should I, and I do, mostly. But, dear Lord, don't make me have to go to another country or stick out my neck in my own to prove it.

In the name of fleas, I made a couple of enemies today, and I am scared at just how far I'll have to go to fight them. The Japanese dog got fleas after he came here; his owners can't understand the instructions on how to fight them; the people I asked to help them said no.

No. My dad was in World War II. My uncle was a prisoner of war. They are taking jobs from our kind. They are marrying, diluting our kind. They are buying up our land. No.

Should I put my byline on the story or not? Can you believe this is me asking you this? Me, the fearless reporter? Me, champion of the underdog, no pun intended? Will people be angry with me for introducing our new residents in such a friendly, benevolent way? Will they add me to their list of "suspicious" liberals? Will I get a letter to the editor?

Go with me, Lord, back to that store to pick up the flea spray. Hold back my anger lest that become an excuse for others to dismiss me. Help me understand how families pass down grievances along with flat feet and bald heads. Help me to be a bridge builder, not a bomber with my words. Without your steadying hand, I can see me—many of us—becoming the very thing we deplore: prejudiced.

Help me to find a balance between being righteously

indignant on another's behalf and a self-righteous pick-eter whose focus is on winning, having lost sight of the cause. Help me to find ways to ease the introductions of people in a world grown too small to be strangers. For there is little room left in which to hide. And so many of those we label strangers are in such terrible need. How can we say, "Go away"?

Help me to put aside battles, then, users of energy, so that I can become a friend to this stranger. And, if you decide that I should venture in a far country, assure me that I won't be alone. Send me a friend, a dove like I tried to be today, showing that you really do love all the little children of the world, never mind who threw the first bomb.

37

Magnolia

He would've grown a beard had he thought of it in time. As it was, no socks, untied moccasins, and a brazenly tilted mortar board were the best last-minute protests he could wage. For today's ending snuck up on him, and he'd come to college graduation unprepared.

I was prepared, however, with a rare treasure in the car to crown this day. I could hardly wait to share it with a family that's seen very few.

A magnolia.

My namesake flower, she is a gracious southern belle, her springtime fragrance hinting of juleps, bluegrass, croquet on the lawn, and of my childhood where she spoke my name: Margaret Anne, Maggie, Mag, Magnolia, I've answered to them all.

They seldom survive where I live now, and I always miss their pageantry, since my family visits usually coincide with fall's gently burning beauty in the Smoky Mountains.

This year I went in spring. Essence of honeysuckle was a herald announcing the queen of the plantation ball through the open car windows as we drove over the dark mountains. Arriving at our motel, I sniffed around the midnight parking lot like hound after fox. I'd not expected the magnolias to be on hand to welcome me home.

"There's one!" I exclaimed the next morning as we passed first one then another of the blossoming trees at their peak. Later, visits done, on the way home via a son's graduation, I left a nosegay of sassy red carnations on Mother's grave, surprised how her weathered headstone had grown to look as if it belonged with ancestors resting nearby. Caretaker over them all stood dozens of forty- to sixty-foot magnolia trees.

I just couldn't resist.

I plucked a mostly opened blossom, savoring its fragrance as I wrapped it in a napkin. Hesitating, I envisioned it wilting long before I was ready to relinquish it. So, why not take a bud? A water fountain in a nearby mall filled a discarded pickle jar to put both blossom and bud in; a polystyrene cooler carried them to graduation.

From my hard concrete seat in the stadium, I thought about them as I set the evening's graduation-dinner table in my mind, magnolias center stage. Now, a son occupied that place of honor despite his grief at leaving this home away from home, friends now like family. It felt good to be there reclaiming him.

Against a bruised bank of gathering thunderclouds, hordes of seventeen-year locusts sang a cappella accompaniment for commencement speakers, adding pomp to his bittersweet circumstance. He was only four years old the last time the locusts sang, I realized, tallying the years in between. I swallowed hard against their passing with each step he took across the stage, the locusts echoing his name. He'll be nearly forty years old when they sing for him again, I told him as we walked to the car later.

The anguished look he returned me in exchange for

my quick spending of his life shushed any more forecasts of a future he saw as frightening for him and his classmates who were, they'd begun to suspect in those last few weeks of college, really still playmates.

A few had arrived at their objectives and received briefcases for graduation; others were trading cap and gown for wedding finery the next day; still others, like this child standing man-tall beside me at the car, only knew they didn't know what to do next.

His room at home is always welcome, we assured him. Hometown jobs were available if not lucrative. Take time to think, to consider, to relax and coast awhile, we suggested while helping him move from his college room. Come, let us take care of you, we hinted. My mothering arms promised comfort, sanctuary, and he seemed relieved.

I'm still needed, I fairly sang on the way home from the campus.

His favorite foods gathered around the elegant dinner centerpiece, my fragrant magnolia blossom. I saved the bud in the refrigerator.

As I'd known it couldn't, the blossom didn't last, scarcely holding up its head past dessert; a few creamy petals browned and fell on the table over coffee. I set it aside to dry, planning to use its filled seed cone and leaves in a dried arrangement. Could a seedling grow here if planted in full sun? I wondered, deciding to experiment.

From its safe place in the wings, the bud was retrieved to take the place of honor. There, it remained closed and strangely unfragrant. I watched it for several days: It never did anything. Neither opening, wilting, nor smelling, it just sat. Finally, I threw it and its stunted seed cone — no good even for a decoration — into the trash amidst leftovers tossed by our graduate as he prepared to leave home after all.

He didn't need what I offered. Stung, I launched earnest tugs-of-war over what was best for him. He had no questions, really, that leaving was best. He also had no job, no plans, no graduate school commitments to comfort me, I retorted, yearning for days when mothering was a bandage here, a hug there, a lap on which to smooth away a child's pain. And now this child was asking me to let him have his pain, to take it on the road with him so he could see if his own is lap enough for himself.

When they finally stand up, side by side with a child, mothers can make their laps disappear, folding them neatly into comfortable memories, into roots from which to spring.

He cleaned his closet, stored his books, and got a job 2,000 miles away. I cooked favorite meals, copied favorite recipes to send along, and tried to quit answering questions he never asked.

The full magnolia blossom, now drying in the basement, deeply enjoyed, was so quickly gone. Gone like childhood, like college years, like locust songs, like bandage strips. The bud protected and saved, however, had never become what it could have been, clutched as it was too tightly in the fear of its being lost.

Last week, I filled paper cups with dirt and carried them out to the sunny porch steps within view of the graduate as he carried his life-in-a-backpack belongings to the waiting car. A bike strapped on top promised side-road adventures in Glacier mountains circled on his map.

Chatting idly as he loaded up, I hulled and planted the seeds from the cone of the fully bloomed flower that had passed so quickly. So quickly passed, yet its yield is the only one capable, bound, to grow on.

A mother's harvest is a child grown too full not to go ahead and bloom. Tears of farewell, my son, are only a brief spring shower.

Prayer

Uncertainties, Lord, clump like cold oatmeal in the pit of my stomach as I hear him pitching and tossing things about in his room. A guest room, it will become, I suspect.

He's been hard on the carpet, the woodwork, and marks on the ceiling are a soft-basketball backboard. At least now I can repaint and wallpaper without hesitation. Perhaps blue.

How can I think about colors at a time like this, Lord, a time when my only son is leaving home? A time when I'll have to quit being a mother, I fear. So, I'll become a decorator, right? Pure defense, Lord, changing the subject.

We've quit fighting now, which is a relief for us both. But I don't relent well, do I, Lord, in my certainty that I know what is best? Yet, he's right: What difference does it make if I do know what's best?

None.

For my knowledge is not his, nor are my answers to questions I'm the only one asking.

It's easy for you to let him go, I challenged my husband, penalizing him for all primitive maleness that sends sons and their sons and theirs forever away from home unto the umpteenth generation.

He just held me, Lord, as I feel you doing, too. A mother relinquishing a son to himself is a pitiful sight, and I am ashamed. I thought I knew better, Lord, and certainly credited myself as wearing long apron strings. As a matter of fact, I've boasted that I'm a modern mother, one who wears no apron at all.

But I am suddenly clutching apron strings so tightly all circulation is cut off. No wonder my son and I are stuck; there's no trust flowing, lifeblood strong, between us. There's no assumption, either, of your companionship with us both. In my fear, I've forgotten you can go in both directions at once.

Forgive my sudden fright, my regrets at having encouraged his independence, his strength. Forgive my tight-fisted mothering.

So, look at me, Lord, as one by one I'm unclenching my fingers around his life I'd mistakenly thought to best protect by holding on at the last minute. One by one, too, I'm counting the freckles on his handsome face, which is happiest when he's telling me his dreams. And, be ready, Lord, for one by one I'm marking off the days you and I will have to walk to the mailbox before there are the cards he promises to send. One by one, each step he and I take apart will keep us close in ways that free us both.

Thank you, Lord, for the gift of distance I welcome, too, when I'm honest. For I'm ready to go on, too. My lap, happily empty of children, is now filling with manuscripts, with letters to scattered kids, with concert and play programs enjoyed with a special husband.

Thank you, too, for the common trait of stubbornness this son and I share that wouldn't let us part without a truce. Thank you for postcards, his next link to me.

Not losing a son, I'll explain to the paint store clerk, I'm gaining a spare bedroom painted blue: a son's favorite color. The exact tint? About the shade of a biking-trail blue sky or an ocean wave. About the shade of space.

38

Bang! You're Dead

Sighting down the barrel of the .357 magnum, I squeezed the trigger and blew the man away.

Bull's eye.

Researching a story on women against crime, I was enrolled in a gun-and-safety course taught by the local police. The "man" was my bullet-riddled target whose mortal head-and-heart wounds earned me marksmanship scores.

Later that afternoon, deadline met, I left for a week-long church seminar, "Blessed are the Peacemakers." My lifesize cardboard assailant rode contentedly beside me in the car, a "show and tell."

How, I wondered aloud to him, are we to reconcile violence with peacemaking; defense with offense; protection with vulnerability and trust? How can we dare turn the other cheek, much less our back, on those who consider us objects, not people?

We live in dreadful times when to turn the other cheek is to risk its being slashed, too. To be a Samaritan is often to fall into a carefully baited trap. A young mother who lived not far from here stopped to help a "stranded" motorist; her brutalized body and those of her two young children were found in a dried-up creek bed months later, a metaphor for our times. Why list more horror stories, for don't we all have at least one to tell?

It was relief to bask in a week of peace-considering conversation and classes; a sad shock to return to the "real world" with a local rapist terrorizing neighborhoods, and my uneasiness about how well I had handled a gun.

Should I buy a gun for protection, as advised? I worried. I'd proven myself capable of using it safely and more or less skillfully. And I knew there were times, were I in danger, that I'd not hesitate to follow the trajectory I'd learned: Shoot to do damage if not kill.

And then the Ribbon of Peace came to town.

Ten miles long at the time it arrived on our county's boundaries, the Ribbon of Peace had been conceived by a Colorado woman who had wondered about war and its aftermath. "What would I not want to live without?" For, she had come to understand, that this time, if there were to be war, the stakes would be high — too high.

So, she suggested her bit of "foolishness," as she called it at first, to a few friends and relatives, urging them to create word pictures for a Ribbon of Peace. Perhaps they could come up with a mile of panels, symbols of what they could not bear to lose through nuclear war, the ultimate violence, the "big gun."

"This will be a gentle reminder that we love the earth and its peoples," she explained.

The ribbon, created eventually by hundreds of women across the United States, stopped by here enroute to a peace march around the Pentagon, across the Potomac River, and then a circle around the White House in a memorial for the bombing of Hiroshima and Nagasaki.

Here, I sighed in relief as I wrote an assigned news story about the ribbon and its local contributors, was my solution. Peace is the answer, my story is my statement.

I reported about the prayer vigils to be held at the courthouse for anyone who wanted to stop by; about the ribbon as backdrop for a Memorial Day program to be held on the courthouse lawn liberally planted with white crosses to honor our war dead.

Peace amidst chaos even on deadline, I thought.

And then the hate mail hit my desk, and letters to the editor hit his.

Radical, commie lover, flag burner, unpatriotic were a few of the labels heaped on my journalistic head and that of the minister who conducted the Memorial Day service, where he mentioned the ribbon as a symbol of hope that "we will make war no more," big wars or little wars.

From peace to violence in one fell swoop.

I felt vulnerable again, not so much because of criticism of my article, which comes with the territory, but because of its tone, a reminder that a local company on strike had threatened many people, including reporters; that the rapist had struck again; that I drove down a dark street to get to work at night; that not everyone believes in peace, but rather in victory.

The minister who shared the hot seat with me had served in the armed forces and was present at the site of the signing of the peace treaty at the end of World War II. He'd buried many young men lost in Vietnam. In his letter of response to the critics, he suggested that to honor the war dead, we owe them a pledge to work for peace lest they have died in vain.

"The point is," he explained, "we must achieve peace or there won't be any point."

And, as the song, and my story's lead, pointed out, "Let there be peace on earth, and let it begin with me."

But I still wasn't comfortable with how to defend myself peacefully. A paradox if there ever was one, because isn't it equally true that if our fellow citizens act as if they have a right not to behave and to mug and attack us, then we have a right to defend ourselves?

A problem to sleep on, which I did, but with one ear open: The rapist was still at large, his last attack leaving a husband who'd tried to intervene in a coma from head injuries he'd received for his gallantry. The woman had still been raped.

It was a sultry, sticky and humid summer night, typical of our Hoosier summers. We didn't have central air conditioning, and the area floor fans only half-heartedly swept hot air back and forth.

I was finally deeply asleep, when a sound on the screened porch right outside the bedroom awakened me. I knew in that moment I'd made a mistake in not buying, loading, and now having within a hand's quick reach the pistol I'd been offered.

Terrified, I began screaming in lieu of shooting, which I would most certainly have done . . . and would do, I vowed, if I got out of this alive. A large shape loomed in the door from the porch and staggered into our room.

My husband, jolted awake by my screams, and I leaped from bed to attack . . . our son.

Our son.

Not an intruder, but a teenager who, unable to sleep in his hot room, had taken blankets and pillow through the other door onto the porch to catch what breezes there were. Mosquitoes had chased him in, he explained, by this time as frightened as we, for he thought, from our reactions, someone was behind him.

Our son. But as I looked at his dear, sleepy face in the light, all I could see overlaid upon it was the silhouette of my bull's-eye-pocked target. I was too good to have missed and too frightened to have asked questions first.

Peace on earth—and my gamble with the odds of

violence—began that night. My target, thumbtacked on the utility room wall, and I greet one another daily. Proof that I can shoot to kill; a reminder that I won't.

Prayer

A stranger came to my door yesterday, Lord, and I turned him away, locking the door as fast as I could.

And today we installed new bolts.

How can I recognize any of your needful creatures, Lord, when I see menace in every outstretched hand? How can I find peace and not be anxious for the 'morrow when our daughters are traveling cross-country alone this weekend, our son wants to hitchhike to the northwest this summer, and we both recall our sudden summer fright? Thank you for my procrastination that had prevented me from having bought a gun.

It makes me so angry, Lord, to be afraid in my own home, my own community. But today I reported on a woman raped down our road. A friend was abducted and locked in her own car's trunk for hours, and the abductor will be free to come after her again next month.

Where were you then, Lord? Will you be there when I need you? Do you want us to barricade ourselves? Shall we take up arms against the enemy, no matter how many innocent get caught in the crossfire?

What about those who see peace as the greater enemy, who see patriotism and strength as only attack and victory over the current enemy, and see defeat in every negotiation? Sometimes I feel I must arm myself against them!

Yet, often Lord, I suspect that the enemy lurks within all of us and our taste for violence, our rage against those not quite like us. We entertain ourselves, too, by vicariously killing and maiming, feeling powerful through the heroes we create.

Lord, most of all, reassure me that the senseless attacks can be redeemed, that the broken, battered, and violated can be cleansed and able to walk outside again. Send them your comfort.

And be with us as we wrestle with how to be armed peacemakers. Help us reclaim our world—for living in, not hiding from.

Bless the victims, Lord, the actual ones as well as those who live the assaults in their dread, their nightmares.

39

A Fish Story

Reversing summer's routine, I withdrew my daily plea for rain, encouraging the drought to continue one Saturday longer. At first early morning glance, not a cloud interrupted the horizon's haze. Perfect.

Hamburger stroganoff simmered for lunch, a yogurt pie chilled, as I wrapped birthday packages for two special fellows who shared September birthdays. The older, a twenty-three-year-old son; the younger, a six-year-old I'd never met. If my daughter and his father follow their hearts, he's probably going to be my grandson.

My stepgrandson, a co-worker had corrected, persnickety, earlier in the week.

No big deal, I'd retorted. But I wondered if it were a big deal; already I felt cheated of his first steps, rocking-chair lullabies, baby-spoken "Mammaw" or whatever he might've wanted to call me.

What do you name a fullgrown stepgrandmother? I wondered an hour later as he silently nodded hello.

He sat on his dad's lap during lunch, slipping away briefly to befriend our dogs, who make no distinction between step and nonstep and loved him from the minute he dropped to his knees to hug them. I kept my

distance, my hands busy anywhere but smoothing a strand of blond hair, envying the dogs their place beside him on the couch as he opened his presents.

I'd spent hours roving the toy store aisles, despairing at finding anything that would satisfy both this modern child and my oldfashioned ideas of grandmothering. Stepgrandmothering, I hastily corrected.

It would have to be something easily portable, easily taken between the two halves of his life that had been broken like a candy bar into uneven pieces by divorce. It would have to convey my love, but not expectations of returns.

It, I concluded by my third trip past the bulldozers and dump trucks, would have to convince him how glad I am to be able to know, to grandmother, even stepgrandmother, him without being glad how it happened. Too big a job for a toy; too big a job for even the most well-intentioned stepgrandmother.

For doing too big a job, the tiniest cars were made—tiny cars, the last aisle over, easy to stash in a pocket as he travels back and forth to his mom's and dad's homes like a gypsy between campfires.

Into his pocket they went, sure enough, weighted down by stones to skip on the river, he explained.

Drought had withered lawns, stunted crops, and shriveled the Big Blue River on whose banks we live. Even its huge resident snapping turtles were despondent, lining the parched banks like sunbathers at low tide.

But he caught a fish anyway.

I'd watched from the porch, camera in hand, as he invited our daughter to help him catch worms and crickets for bait, even letting her hold the jar. Barely flinching, she added to the squirming, jumping critters. This daughter, who, even at twenty-five-years old, still shrieks when unexpected "creepers" cross her path. This daughter, a child of divorce, too, who once caught a trout with her bare hands, grown wise enough to share neither tale with the child. Yet. Time enough to connect lives, dot-to-dot.

This afternoon is just about fishing.

Poles on shoulders, the three of them clambered down the hill to the river almost invisible beyond the trees. "It's pretty low," I cautioned against too-high hopes.

"I think I can still catch a fish for Abigail," he assured me, wanting to share his bounty with the family cat who had wandered in to measure his lap after lunch. Three pirouettes and she'd settled, curled into a circle of comfort for them both. Purring her welcome, she'd dozed as he drove his tiny cars on the plaid lines of the couch, detouring around her dangling white paw.

I heard the fisherfolk before I saw them. An offering outstretched before him, he showed me the fish, tail up in a paper cup sloshing over with river water.

"I think I want to throw him back," he interrupted my congratulations. "Abigail's probably not that hungry. He'd like to be back in the river. He's suffered enough," he continued, a question in his voice.

"Abigail ate some leftovers and then ran into the woods to hunt," I assured him, fingers crossed in hopes the dratted cat wouldn't lug home her frequent baby-rabbit trophies for this tenderhearted child. Not today.

While Dad returned the fish to the river, the child joined me on the porch step. Scooting himself close enough, but no closer, he confessed, "My shoe got wet at the river."

"How squishy," I responded, laughing at the look he returned me. Apparently having passed me on a test I'd not known I was taking, he added shyly, "My foot was in it."

Little boys and rivers are like that, I agreed. It's hard to stay dry, especially when hooks get caught in trees, when the rock a little farther out hints of bigger fish in its shadows, when your foot accidentally slips.

Metal to magnet, little boys go toward water, dirt, fish, tiny cars, and jars of crickets to also be turned loose. To new friends, too, on sunny Saturdays.

Barefooted indoors, his shoe drying on the porch, he discovered a shelf of children's books kept for two decades at just the right height for young readers, the ones our daughter (his stepmother-to-be) loved when she was his age.

"Can we do the riddle book again when I come back?" he asked several stories later.

"Sure," I answered, practicing my best grandmother line, no need to step around our need for one another any longer. "Sure."

Prayer

We have to speak softly today, Lord, for there are dinosaurs sleeping in my purse. I couldn't resist the plastic egg filled with green creatures, just the right size to fit a small boy's hand, smooth and cool. I'm saving them for just the right time.

He seems to like me even without little gifts, which is a relief, for I worry that I might be too loud, too enthusiastic, for him. I forget that he is mourning in the midst of my celebrating. He's lost a daily dad, and no grandmother, step or not, can make up for that. No way.

Touch him with comfort, Lord, in a summer breeze as soft as today's to comb back his blond hair; wrap him in your first winter snowfall as tight and safe in its blanket as the family he once knew. Bless him with the courage to try new traditions, new relatives, new homes. Fuel and empower him in his rage, easing him with the assurance that his rage is okay, his tears healing, that he has the strength to live in two worlds, that comfort comes to those who dare mourn.

Help me to be loving to him with no strings attached; to simply let him come and go in my life taking only what he needs, not what I need to give.

For, impatient, I keep answering the question no one has asked: Yes, I'd love to be his grandmother. Keep me still and quiet; keep me from blurting out too much too soon; from trying to bandage hurts simply because I can't watch or life doesn't seem fair; from touching his pain, or allegiance, before he's ready.

Let me be content to be a sunny-Saturday-afternoon snapshot taped to his dad's refrigerator, a silly-riddle-book lady, a place it's okay to get shoes wet. A purse where dinosaurs hibernate.

Help me to cradle this child's trust even as I would have his infant body had I been so fortunate. Thank you for bringing us together over even the smallest things: dinosaurs, riddles, rivers.

I know it would've been a wonderful day even if it had rained, or if the river had been completely dried up, but, dear Lord, thank you for the fish.

40

Hinges

The gate between the reception area and newsroom swung both ways beneath my shoving hip. To and fro. Back and forth. It had never done that before, and even with my hands full of boxes and files, like a delighted child I stood in the newsroom after a six-month's absence watching the gate swing.

A child at play, I chuckled, glad no one was there to see my foolishness, one of the best souvenirs I'd brought back from my sabbatical.

Sabbatical: "a recurring period of rest given at intervals." Last year I'd negotiated a sabbatical from my reporter/family editor job to accompany my husband on his from the church. On the burnout scale, we were cinders, we tried to explain jokingly to any who would listen.

Burnout: is there any need to define this word? Probably not, for there are as many versions and symptoms of this modern malady as there are frantic, overworked, overbusy, and overburdened people.

I'd thought I just needed a break from routine, ringing telephones, and deadlines. It wasn't until the middle of the sabbatical that I diagnosed my own dis-ease:

burnout. Rereading my journal, I see the symptoms in bold, neon, billboard-tall words.

Day One. I only managed to stop and pull the weeds running rampantly along the driveway. I didn't even notice the flowers, much less realize I now had time to smell them. Not a story idea was left in my shrunken thoughts; ideas were sluggish, and spring's freshness mocked them.

Day Two dawned the triple crown of frenzy: Mother's Day; a daughter's twenty-sixth birthday and seminary commencement; bon voyage for a son heading for summer work in Maine and for another daughter off to a summer of study in England. Everyone was in transition, movement. When did this get to be a grown-up family? Who would we all be in four months when we'd be reunited? I was too rusty, too stiff in spirit and body, to do more than shuffle behind them, my joints creaking protest with every step.

Day Three. I discovered a bluebird in the backyard that appeared to have a nest. I must research and see if they live here in summers. Two weeks later, I was still convinced I was overwhelmed, still felt deadlines that punched with time-clock regularity in my gut. I couldn't flow with the unwinding of the day itself . . . must fast forward it.

Day Fifteen. I awoke in a sweat, my hand on the clutch, my foot on the brake. What a crazy dream. I had pulled to a stop in a parking lot, put the car in "park," and turned off and removed the key. Yet the engine kept running. Even I couldn't miss the message in that. How was I to slow the racing of my internal combustion yet speed up and unbind my stiff spirit?

The bluebird offered me a hint that day: Just enjoy my hide-and-seek games among the sycamore leaves, he seemed to advise, flying about so delightfully that I dared not get up from the porch rocker and find something else to do for fear of missing him. Not do research and make the bird a task; just wait and see whether he stays or migrates on? New thought.

Why rush? we finally asked ourselves in the midst of cramming too much into days of preparation to leave town. Can't the unwinding begin today? Now, this very minute? Closing the door firmly on unpacked suitcases and unfinished lists, we went hiking.

Day Twenty-five. We arrived in Princeton, New Jersey. Husband's alma mater, Princeton Seminary, greeted us across the street from our student digs, which we shared with a young Korean couple and their toddling son. The language barrier reduced us to mostly smiles and patchwork conversations.

Day Thirty-seven. Homesickness must be in the water, for I missed my plants, my dogs and cat, the bluebird; and, dare I confess, my too-tight schedule? Annoyed at first by the intruding sounds from across the hall, I listened more closely. A soul-sung melody drew me to open our door to better hear the young father's homesick lullaby to a fretful child. It was a church-camp sort of song, vaguely familiar; he sang each verse once in Korean, once in English. We were all a bit displaced, and I hummed my own descant of wistfulness.

I finally quit counting the days.

Writing, talking, walking, reading, napping, walking, talking, writing . . . the days developed lives of their own, punctuated with replenishing tourist wanderings as well as draughts of silence and meditation. Whether in daily quiet times or worship, the high-ceilinged stone chapel easily contained my runaway thoughts that still ricocheted inside my mind. I claimed the round table third from center in the seminary library, and did what I've always wanted to do: write until I was ready to quit. Pulled an all-nighter, too, writing until I was done. Delicious freedom, and I gently flexed my rusty spirit to see if I was still stuck in overdrive. Sluggish response; good sign.

Last day in Princeton. We couldn't pack the car, though, for the Korean woman sat, maybe in labor with her second child, on our bottom step. Politely she'd shaken her head at our offer of help and she sat patiently cradling the unborn child in her lap. Stalling as long as we could, we finally had no choice but to retreat upstairs and not intrude. Her husband had gone for the car, she pantomimed. An unfinished story; was it a boy or girl? Who will help her with two little ones?

Horse thieves used to be shot, a practice I heartily endorsed, at least momentarily. We were robbed, one of seven cars at the motel broken into our first night on the road. Everything was stolen: manuscript notes, computer, clothes, mementos, books, a basketball, tapes. A violation, and we shuddered in horror and shook with rage. This, however, will not be the last word about the sabbatical, we vowed. How precious is our safety? Beyond measure, we concluded as we tallied up our material losses, paltry in comparison with what could've been. Trite, tried words are the truest: Each day is a gift.

Back home again in Indiana. Is there any place as lush and lovely as the Midwest in late summer? The dogs were ecstatic at our return, the cat a twisting, twining circle of greeting around our ankles. The bluebird was gone.

We had to begin counting days again, but this time forward to a daughter's wedding day; weed, mulch, smooth new gravel in driveway, plant a few mums for spot color, pick a few for my desk. Newly acquired patience and calm, however, got sorely tested as the wedding day drew nearer and lists longer. I could see serenity a fading blip on a radar screen that measured my frustration. A good laugh, a hike in the woods, and a new haircut intervened before all was lost. It'll get done.

Wedding Day. A lizard eyed the punch bowl at the wedding reception on our screened porch the day I became a stepgrandmother. Dressed in bright blue "tails," how did it know that blue was the bride's favorite color? Poised politely still and apparently serene on the little boy's hand, it was a most welcome guest on this bittersweet day for a new-suited stepgrandson, who gently carried his new pet in and out of the house. Carefully releasing the critter beneath the sidewalk when it was time to leave, he told it good-bye, promising to check for it when he comes back. Comes back, wonderful words of love. I've never been so happy to be taken for granted, I told the slithery lizard when I encountered it taking a sunbath the next week. Each day I straighten a story this proud first grader wrote for my refrigerator, a story of a fat cat, a bat, and a rat, all who sat on a hat . . . on a mat. A literary genius, my stepgrandson.

Reluctantly I found myself counting days again, but to savor and spend, not hoard and begrudge their passing. Day 146. We dug a small fire pit in our side yard and roasted bratwursts, marshmallows, and toes around its embers. Overhead, leaves hem-hawed before gently letting go and falling around us like story ideas slowly peeking around margins of my imagination.

Day 151. Snowstorm. Beautiful flakes sifted onto the still-colorful leaves outside my window. Snow in October? I'm dreaming of a white Halloween, I sang. It was a treat for this southern gal who's not lost her delight in the first snowfall of each season. Tuck this postcard scene away as a resource to take with me in a pocket of memory for hectic days just ahead, I reminded myself.

Day after day we worked outside again, each fall day more glorious and unexpected than the previous, for how long could this returned Indian summer last?

I refinished an old—circa 1810—nine-foot-long walnut work table with deep drawers for bills and story ideas, then rearranged my home office around it for a new view and easier movement: a metaphor in walnut. Across its one-board top is scrawled the journal of my table: clothing pattern tracing wheel marks; holes for attaching food grinder, apple peeler, sausage stuffer. Like the Indians who are claimed in legend to be present in the hazy smoke that spreads over the autumn hills, the table's previous users greeted me with each morning cup of tea; the table reeks of their tales that hover over its worn surface. Maybe they know a good yarn or two they'll impart one winter evening. I think I've slowed down enough to listen.

Days. I lost count again, as there were so few left before returning to job and routine. Was I different? Restored, balanced, and energized? More trusting and relaxed? Like settling into a hammock strung between trees, it's hard when facing change, even such positive change, not to dangle an anchoring foot outside; faith, like balance, is difficult to achieve.

The inevitable day arrived, and I moved back into the silent, off-duty newsroom through this free-moving gate. Desk reloaded, phone lists and appointment book updated, I was ready to swing it wide that first Monday morning; each new day followed quickly and busily on its heels.

Like my compulsions and circumstances that confined and defined me, the newsroom gate originally had a wooden stop that held it fast against full movement. After years of pinched fingers, stubbed shins, and collisions with a one-direction gate, someone finally realized that all it would take for more efficient, convenient, and safe operation was simply a set of new hinges.

How long, I laugh as I still fumble awkwardly through it, will it take before I realize that I can push or pull the gate in my comings and goings? Momentarily stuck midswing in my old habits, I'm always surprised that it now moves so freely beneath my hand.

Prayer

O Lord of shrinkings and stretchings, of stops and starts, of exits and entrances, of comings and goings, I celebrate your gift of movement. And, Lord of rainy afternoons and quilt-covered naps, I also celebrate your gift of stillness. Thank you for forging the two into renewing links of balance for me.

How long had you been seeking me, Lord, before I recognized your hints in the headaches of mind and body that finally got my attention and halted me in midstride? It is hard for even you to hit a moving target, Lord, and I raced pell-mell through life always just out of reach of your calmness. Yet it is the gift I yearned for the most even as I darted after it.

Thank you for teaching this old dog new tricks of relaxation in leisurely walks and talks with myself, with companions, and especially with you. Thank you for the excitement I again feel at the glimpse of a story idea dangling like a loose thread at the edge of my imagination that had grown cloudy like an old fish bowl.

Thank you for the newest lives I have been able to greet with open, steadier hands: that fisherman now a stepgrandchild who swaps riddles with me and writes stories for my refrigerator; that steadfast, loving son-in-law who has never been a stranger.

Thank you for renewed connections with the oldest, most familiar lives I have energy to celebrate anew as they cross wide-spanning bridges these days: that long-distance bicycling son writing stories on the rocky coast of Maine; that daughter ordering her college cap and gown and setting a life course on an international compass; that daughter, a wife and stepmother, weaving a family and risky, care-giving vocation; that husband making a Christmas batch of sawdust in his shop.

I know them differently these days, Lord, as tiny moving shards in a kaleidoscope blown about by your creative spirit that is constantly shifting us.

Continue to breathe new life, Lord—just a gently moving breeze instead of the gales I used to crave—through my soul each day. Continue to provide for me the second wind I need just to take the next step, a sufficient distance.

Touch my shoulder with a tolerant hand of restraint if I start to bolt toward some new adventure or after some worry before thinking it through. Open my eyes some days, Lord, to the glorious possibilities that are mine; shut them in rest on other days, Lord, in lunchtime naps.

When I begin jumping up and down in one spot or pacing circles into ruts around myself, Lord, nudge me to seek the contentment of a child swinging slowly on the garden gate, to and fro, in arcs of free motion. Your presence is oil enough for my hinges.